Communication Style

A Beginner's Guide on Effective Communication in Life and Work

Kevin Jobson

or indirect, that are incurred as a result of the use of the information contained within this document, including, but not limited to, errors, omissions, or inaccuracies.

Table of Contents

INTRODUCTION 1

CHAPTER 1: COMMUNICATION IN THE WORKPLACE 5

KNOW YOURSELF AS AN EMPLOYEE 7
    Strengths and Weaknesses 7
    Personality 9
KNOW YOUR COLLEAGUE/BOSS/SUBORDINATE 11
    Strengths and Weaknesses 11
    Personality 12
    Know Your Company's Ethos 13

CHAPTER 2: COMMUNICATION IN ROMANTIC RELATIONSHIPS 15

KNOW YOURSELF AS A PARTNER 16
    Strengths and Weaknesses 16
    Personality 17
YOUR NEEDS 18
KNOW YOUR PARTNER 20
    Strengths and Weaknesses 20
    Personality 21
    Their Needs 22
UNDERSTAND HOW THIS KNOWLEDGE IMPACTS COMMUNICATION 24

CHAPTER 3: PLANNING TO SEND 27

DECIDE ON WHAT TYPE OF COMMUNICATION IS BEST SUITED TO THE SITUATION 27
    Face to Face 28
    In Writing 29
    One on One 30
    Group Address 31
ADAPTING YOUR COMMUNICATION STYLE TO YOUR AUDIENCE 31
    Make Them Feel Comfortable 33

CHAPTER 4: SENDING 37

COMMUNICATION STYLES 37
    Passive 38
    Aggressive 40
    Passive-Aggressive 43
    Assertive 45

CHAPTER 5: RECEIVING **49**

RECEIVING WITH YOUR EARS 50
    Focusing on the Speaker 50
    Avoiding Interruptions 51
    Show Encouragement 52
    Clarify If You're Not Sure 54
RECEIVING WITH YOUR EYES 55
    Be Aware of Cultural Differences 55
    Consider All Nonverbal Cues Together—Don't Jump to Conclusions Based on One 56

CHAPTER 6: THE POWER OF PERSUASION **59**

The Principle of Reciprocity 59
The Principle of Consistency and Commitment 61
The Principle of Social Proof 62
The Principle of Liking 63
Authority 64
Scarcity 66
A Word of Caution 67

CHAPTER 7: BARRIERS TO EFFECTIVE COMMUNICATION **69**

STRESS AND/OR EMOTION 69
RESISTANCE TO CHANGE 72
LACK OF FOCUS 74
BODY LANGUAGE 75
CULTURAL BARRIERS 76

CHAPTER 8: DIFFICULT CONVERSATIONS **79**

PLANNING FOR A DIFFICULT CONVERSATION 79
DEALING WITH UNPLANNED DIFFICULT CONVERSATIONS 80
THE BASIC RULES 82
    Being Empathic 82
REFERRING TO 'I' NOT 'YOU' 83
    Finding Common Ground 85
UNDERSTANDING YOUR TRIGGERS 86

CONCLUSION **89**

REFERENCES **93**

Introduction

All conscious people communicate in one form or another, whether by talking, writing, signing, crying, or even just grunting. This comes naturally and doesn't require any special teaching skills. A baby automatically knows to cry to signify its discomfort, whether it be a wet diaper, hunger, pain, or tiredness. Nobody teaches it to do that. This is the most basic form of communication, but certainly not the most effective. Ask any young parent who has a crying baby. How many times have you heard them say to their crying bundle, "what's wrong?" or "I wish you could talk!"? Parents are left to try and work out, by process of elimination, which issue needs attention. The same applies to educated adults who are fully capable of talking and writing. They still don't necessarily communicate effectively.

It is important to note that effective communication is a two-way process. It involves both sending (speaking, writing, or signing) and receiving (listening). In order to communicate effectively, you need to focus on both. You would be surprised at how many people don't manage this process well.

Think about it. Have you ever heard someone say "please don't put me next to Jane, she talks too much"? What they're actually saying (over and above the obvious) is Jane doesn't listen! I'm sure we all know a 'Jane'; the person who asks you a question in the middle of a long story, but as you open your mouth to answer, they launch into the next chapter without pausing. You put up with this type of behavior politely for a while, eventually tuning out and hoping that you're nodding and smiling at the right time. At the first available opportunity you turn to your neighbor and engage them in conversation—any conversation— just to escape being monopolized and "talked at" for the whole event.

Our theoretical Jane is an ineffective communicator, and is usually totally unaware of it, because people are too polite to tell her.

Ineffective communication can, as in Jane's case, make you socially awkward and result in you being excluded from some invitations, or being placed at the table with all the most boring and socially awkward friends or colleagues. While that's not fun, it's not a disaster. But it could be.

Poor communication has been responsible for countless catastrophes. Marriages have irretrievably broken down because one partner didn't express their needs properly and then resented the other for not being caring of those needs. Others have felt unloved because their spouse never says "I love you," not because they don't love their partner, but because to them it is a no-brainer. They think that the fact that they married you, committed their life to you—forever—is proof positive of that love and it doesn't need to be reiterated every five minutes. This can leave a partner who needs affirmation feeling like the bottom has fallen out of their world.

Siblings have cut each out of their lives because of a strong difference of opinion, causing enormous heartache to the rest of the family who love them both. Many times, with proper communication you find out later that there was in fact not such a vast difference in opinion. One or both of them simply expressed themselves badly, or was not open to listening to the other point of view, and eventually emotion and anger took over, creating a permanent rift.

On the work front, bad communication can result in you being disciplined unnecessarily, overlooked for a promotion, or even worse, dismissed from a job that you love. This can be because you have communicated your needs or ambitions poorly, were unable to get the best out of your colleagues or team, or even because your boss had not provided clear parameters of what they expected of you. Have you ever felt overwhelmed and inadequate at work? Most people have, and quite often it's not because they are not capable of carrying out the task, but rather that they have not been given the tools or guidelines to set them on the correct path. Imagine being fired because of poor performance when actually the boss was a poor communicator! While you can't wave a magic wand and turn your boss into a good one, this book will teach you not only how to communicate well yourself, but how to draw the right information out of others and get them to provide you with the information that you need to succeed.

In business, lucrative deals have been lost because of communication errors. In the simplest form, it might be a tender deadline that was overlooked or not properly communicated to a member of the team. In more complex cases, not understanding the needs of the client (whether it's your fault or theirs) can create misunderstandings and unhappiness, losing you a valuable client and potentially damaging your reputation if that client expresses that unhappiness on social media or to other clients or potential clients.

Don't be that person! Don't be the one who is always being misunderstood and unappreciated. Don't let trivial misunderstandings fester and escalate into unsurmountable problems. With the right tools, you can take control. You can turn bad situations into good, make people you care about happy and give others confidence in you. You can strengthen your relationships, improve your career prospects, and even improve your financial situation—all through effective communication.

By reading this book you will learn not only how to express yourself effectively at home and in the workplace, but also how to listen properly. You will discover how to listen to more than the spoken word, to read non-verbal signs (body language) and better understand the message. You will also learn how to draw information out of people who are not good communicators, as well as how to use communication to gain empathy and strengthen your own powers of persuasion.

Communicating effectively is not just about the exchange of words or ideas, it's about understanding and being understood. It's the cornerstone of building amazing relationships and succeeding in every avenue of life.

Chapter 1:

Communication in the Workplace

Like any form of communication, communication in the workplace has a number of elements that contribute to its success or failure. The two main elements are the speaker (or writer) and the listener (or reader).

The next element is the context of the situation. This can be further broken down into three categories. Firstly, the method (e.g. an email, letter, speech, informal discussion, group debate, one on one conversation, etc.) which will be discussed later in Chapter 4. Secondly, the purpose of the communication, what you're going to say (e.g. are you making an announcement, discussing a sensitive issue, brainstorming, or even explaining a problem). The purpose of your communication will influence your choice of method, more of this is also in Chapter 4. Thirdly, the nature of the people participating and their relationship.

In this chapter we explore a combination of the two main elements and the last element. We look at both participants in the communication and their relationship, both with each other and with the company. You need to understand yourself and how you typically react to situations, emotions, or people, so that you can manage your reactions and responses. What irritates you and why, what are you good at and what do you struggle with? Knowing this about yourself will help you to manage your communication, avoid misunderstandings, and get people on your side.

Just as importantly, you need to understand your audience; the person or people that you are talking to. If you know what makes them happy, what frustrates them and what motivates them, you can plan what you are going to say and how you are going to say it in a way that will get you the best possible results.

Then you need to consider your relationship with the person or people you are communicating with. Are you talking to your boss, to a colleague, or to a junior? How you talk to each will be different. I'm not talking about respect here—at work you should aim to be just as respectful to a junior employee as you would be to the CEO—don't swear, get personal, or make demeaning comments to any of them! The cleaner is just as worthy of 'please' and 'thank you' as the boss is. You shouldn't even have to think twice about that. But the expectations of the person you're speaking to may be different. The cleaner probably doesn't expect much of you other than a friendly smile and simple pleasantries. The boss on the other hand, may expect a whole lot more! The boss may expect you to anticipate their or the company's needs, to think for yourself in some instances, and to consult before making decisions in others. You may also have to take a less direct approach with the boss in giving what could be viewed as criticism.

By knowing yourself, your audience, the company ethos, and your relationship with those you are communicating with, you can avoid rubbing people the wrong way, being unduly offended yourself, or losing the sympathy of your listener. You can also get them on your side more easily.

Know Yourself as an Employee

Strengths and Weaknesses

You're probably not going to sit down and analyze yourself before every conversation, but once you've done it for the first time, and you understand yourself, you are unlikely to forget. While most of your strengths and weaknesses will stay the same, some may change over time, especially if you are young or new to your current job, and growing in it; so it's worth doing this exercise once a year or so just to remind yourself of what has changed.

First consider your strengths in relation to the work that you do. Ask yourself, what do I regularly get great feedback on? This could include being:

- punctual
- reliable
- honest
- accurate
- neat
- knowledgeable in a certain area
- focused

This is not a complete list, and you should add to it depending on the type of job you have. Add things to this list that are important for the job that you do, for example, if you're a secretary your typing speed and accuracy might be a strength, or if you're a waiter your ability to remember long or complicated orders might be a strength.

Then, think about your strengths with regard to communication. These could include:

- I get to the point quickly
- I am confident speaking to lots of people

- I make stories interesting and relevant with examples
- I can explain things clearly
- I use humor to make people feel relaxed
- I write well, with good spelling and grammar
- I'm a good listener, people like talking to me
- I'm sensitive to what other people are feeling even if they don't say it

Now do the opposite. Look at your weaknesses, and be brutally honest. The better you know yourself, the better you can plan to take advantage of your strengths and avoid sending mixed messages or making a fool of yourself.

Now consider your weaknesses in your job. What do people criticize about you, or what do you feel you need to improve on? The list below should get you started:

- I'm often late for appointments
- I miss deadlines
- I have to make up stories to cover for mistakes
- I'm always having to re-do work
- I'm untidy (this could be your desk or your handwriting!)
- I'm easily distracted

Then of course your weaknesses in communication:

- I often have to explain things three times before people understand
- I'm shy with strangers or in groups
- I don't like talking, so just stick to the facts
- I don't know how to make things interesting
- I can't seem to express myself clearly in writing—if I talk people understand, but when I send an email people often take things the wrong way
- People never seem to take me into their confidence

- I'm often blindsided by people's reactions, I think I'm just having a heart to heart talk, and then discover that they thought I was being spiteful

You will note that many of these examples are just opposites of the list of strengths. None of them are right or wrong, they are just there to help you understand yourself. If you can't come up with any weaknesses at all, then dig deep. Weaknesses don't have to mean a complete inability to do something, it could just be that you're less good at some things than you are at others. We all have some balance between what comes naturally and what has to be worked at to be achieved—those items that need work would be the ones you need to include as weaknesses.

Personality

Now that you have a list of your strengths and weaknesses, you need to consider your personality. Just like the old saying, "there are three sides to every story, yours, mine, and the truth," there are usually (at least) two versions of a person's personality. There is what you think of yourself and how others see you. In most cases these will be similar, but in some cases they may be very different, especially if people don't know you well. For instance, you may be an extrovert and an entertainer—the life and soul of the party—and if you are, you and those around you are likely to recognize that. But life is often not that simple. You may be a bit of a mixture of extroverted and introverted, and that could change depending on whether you're tired or well rested, or whether you're comfortable with the company you're in, or not.

You probably know yourself well enough, and most people have a fair idea of what others think of them, but it's well worth doing an online personality test if you find it difficult to pinpoint your own character traits. There are a number of tests available, which are usually pretty quick to complete and just involve multiple choice questions. The value of these tests lies in the fact that they give you feedback not only on yourself, but how you relate to others, and how different characteristics can make other people feel.

For instance, if you are someone who puts other people first, many people may see that as a strength, but others may see it as a weakness. They may think that you are not confident enough to stand up for yourself rather than seeing it as pure selflessness. In contrast to this, you may view yourself as a bit of a doormat in situations where others see you as generous and helpful.

Knowing yourself means being aware of your triggers, knowing what motivates you, and what makes you unhappy or angry. This can help you to avoid negative triggers, or to be able to rationalize them to yourself. For example, if your boss says you're always late for deadlines when you've only missed two in your whole life, and it just happened that both occasions were this week. If you know that you get rattled by exaggeration, don't lose your cool and get into a mud-slinging match or try to tell the boss that others do it far more frequently. Tell yourself this person is not saying this to irritate me, it just happens that I react badly to exaggeration. Getting angry is not going to help me to achieve my goal and may make the boss feel defensive about my 'over-reaction,' and then add that to my 'list of sins' so I am going to choose to ignore this trigger. I need to look at the fact that they are expressing and not the way it makes me feel. Imagine how much better the conversation would go if you said, "I know I submitted work late twice this week, and I'm so sorry about it." Then explain why it happened and whether the situation that caused it is resolved or whether or not you need assistance in solving it, for example, time off to deal with personal issues, or help with doing research because you're snowed under.

Know Your Colleague/Boss/Subordinate

Strengths and Weaknesses

It is equally important that you know something about the person or people you are going to be talking to. You'll never know them as well as you know yourself, but you must be able to work out how they fit into the conversation or presentation.

The first thing you need to decide is what the goal of your communication is. Do you want to convince them of something? Do you want to change the way things are done? Do you want them to invest in your idea? Are you trying to motivate them? Do you need support?

In order to work that out, ask yourself two questions: Why am I discussing this subject? What do I need from the person/people I am talking to? This should help you to determine your goal.

Once you have decided on your goal, make a note of the five most important points you are wanting to get across. This will help you to keep your discussion, speech, or email on track.

Now think about the person or people you will be addressing. If it is a junior colleague, the chances are that there may be concepts that they may not understand, which you'll need to describe or explain—or maybe they won't need as much detailed information. Imagine that you are the Information Technology Manager at your firm, and you are going to be talking to your colleagues about internet security. How you approach the subject would differ depending on who you are talking to. Talking to other colleagues in your department would be quick and easy because they'll understand the terminology. But if you were to talk to the elderly accountant who only just knows how to send an email, you might simplify the message, leaving out some of the details about interception fraud, hacking, and spoofing, and focus on just getting the basics across: "Don't trust account details for new suppliers that come via email, these can be messed with, so rather give them a call to confirm that the details are correct before loading them on the internet banking or making a payment."

Perhaps you're going to be talking to the boss about the same subject. You might have other goals, you may want the boss to be careful and adopt new precautions, but you might also like to suggest that the company invests in software to make it less vulnerable. Then you're moving beyond educating the person to help them avoid fraud and wanting to persuade them to spend money to make your job easier. If that's the case, you might want to choose your time carefully and approach the subject differently.

You also need to consider the needs or problems that your audience has. For example, the boss and the accounts department might be more concerned about the company losing money than the receptionist is because they'll have to try to recover the money. You need to think about what they care about and what motivates them. The receptionist might be very busy, and be resistant to the idea of having to make a call to check on bank details when buying something from a new supplier because it takes too long. You need to consider this and point out that you realize it will be a bit of a pain. Maybe providing a simple pre-written WhatsApp that she can send will make her more open to the idea of double checking.

Personality

The personality of the person you are going to be communicating with at work is most important in one on one discussions, or small group discussions. Below are a few scenarios to illustrate this.

If you are going to be wanting to make a change in procedure, you need to be aware of those who are resistant to change. Your approach would be quite different in that situation, in order to get that person's buy in. You will want to lead them to agreeing that the change is necessary, or even help them to 'discover' and suggest the solution themselves. People are often okay with change if it's their own idea, but not so keen on being told to change.

If you need funds for something, but the person you have to get it from is a very cautious spender (or just downright tightfisted!), you need to put more focus on how this will save the company money in the long term.

If you are dealing with an employee related problem, it's wise to know if the person you are going to be speaking to handles criticism well or not. This will tell you whether you can just be direct, or if you need to find a gentler approach.

In addition to knowing something of their personality, in individual cases knowing some of their background can be helpful. Imagine you have an employee who is often late for work, or leaves early, and you need to talk to them about it. If you knew that this person was a single mother with no child support, and doesn't earn enough income to pay for a child minder, you would probably be wise to start with a more cautious and understanding approach, knowing that there might be home reasons that are affecting her ability to stick to rigid times, and you might want to suggest some solutions. However, if the person you're speaking to is a young, single, high-income earner who hangs out at night clubs during the week until all hours, you may decide to take a firmer stance and be less inclined to sympathy.

We will look at how to use this knowledge to your advantage in more detail in Chapter 4.

Know Your Company's Ethos

This is a simple one. In order to do well and progress in the company, you either need to find a company that has the kind of ethos that resonates with you, or be willing to make an effort to adapt to their ethos. It's very easy if you naturally share the principles of the company you work for, but if you don't, your communication style will also have to be adapted to suit the company.

Say your company has an inclusive and democratic ethos, then you would be making a mistake if you approached colleagues with a hardline, saying "This is my department, I'm the boss and I make the decisions, shape up or ship out." That kind of approach may work well in some high-pressure situations in a dog-eat-dog type company, but it's not likely to win you any support in an inclusive and democratic business.

If your company emphasizes environmental awareness, it's probably best not to use your latest trophy hunting trip as an example to make a point. Get to know your company's ethos so that you can avoid unintentionally offending your colleagues, or even worse, your boss with innocent conversation.

Even in casual conversation it is important to be mindful of the company ethos. Some companies (and teams) thrive on high energy, witty comebacks, and playing as hard as you work. Others may be more serious or even more laidback. Imagine if you have come from the first company where slightly risqué jokes about your libido or lifestyle were commonplace over morning coffee, your humor is sharp, and your colleagues love your ribald jokes. Now, you move to a new company, the pay is great, but the people seem serious and the boss adheres to a strict religion. You would definitely need to keep your repartee for home and adopt a gentler, more respectful attitude at work. It's always wise to check out your company's ethos before introducing any of your home life or passions into the workplace. Listen, get a feel for the atmosphere in the office and don't stir things up until you are absolutely sure it's safe to do so. You might think you're being entertaining and lightening the mood, but you might just be offending, and doing your career a whole lot of harm in the process.

Chapter 2

Communication in Romantic Relationships

We all have many different roles in life. We are a child to our parents, parent to our children, a sibling, a friend, a mentor, a colleague, an employee, and a partner or spouse. It is the last of these that we will focus on in this chapter. Many of the tips in this section can also be applied to other social or family relationships, but as the role of partner is the most complicated, it deserves a little extra attention. After all, as long as both parties are living, you will always be a sibling, child, or parent. Being someone's life partner though, involves choice on both sides, so it needs a bit more give and take to make sure that both partners continue to want to be in that partnership. The high divorce rate worldwide is testament to the importance of nurturing your relationship.

Communication within your relationship should not be about who is wrong and who is right, or getting your own way. It should always be rooted in understanding each other and being willing to find middle ground.

Clear and effective communication is probably the single most important tool you have at your disposal to ensure that your partner continues to feel loved and continues to love you and want to be in your life. Like in every form of communication, knowing yourself and knowing the person you're communicating with gives you a huge advantage. Never more so than in a romantic relationship.

Know Yourself as a Partner

Strengths and Weaknesses

Consider your strengths and weaknesses in your home life and in your relationship. Let's start with strengths—they are always so much easier to identify, and will often lead to weaknesses!

Perhaps you are very neat. You don't like to see magazines or glasses standing around. When you walk into a room and see an empty coffee cup, you take it to the kitchen and wash it.

Maybe you are very organized. You keep every invoice and receipt from the shop and file them chronologically. You even put your books and CDs in alphabetical order by author or artist.

Possibly, you are punctual and pride yourself on never being late for anything. It can be very frustrating for a person who is neat, organized, and punctual to have a partner who is laidback, because you are likely to feel that they are making you late and disrupting your lifestyle.

How does this affect your communication? Your feelings and perceptions will almost always affect the way you communicate. You may feel that your partner is a slacker, because they are inclined to "mess up" your shelves and living space and even make you late for events. So when discussing these issues, you may be critical or go on the attack, and it is very likely this will make your partner feel defensive and angry. What is about to come of this is not a discussion, but a heated argument.

It's important to note that your strengths can be perceived by others as weaknesses, and vice versa. Put yourself in your partner's shoes for a moment. Probably one of the things that made you fall in love with them was their relaxed, easy going personality. Consider how they might feel about this discussion. They love you, that's why they got together with you in the first place, and maybe they're just as frustrated by being constantly nagged to keep things clean, neat, and orderly. Maybe they see your strengths as weaknesses in your relationship because you make them feel uncomfortable, whisking away a coffee cup before they've reached the end of the chapter of the book that they were reading, maybe they were planning a second cup.

Knowing your strengths and weaknesses and looking at them from your partner's point of view may just help you to approach such a discussion with more care. Remember that this is a partnership—not a boss-employee, or parent-child, relationship. If you understand your strengths and weaknesses properly you will be able to go into a discussion knowing how you feel, but don't just assume that you are reading the whole situation accurately. Ask your partner how they feel, never assume that you know this. You might think you do, but assumption has been the cause of many disasters (you may know the less polite term that is commonly used, assumption is the mother of all …)

Personality

As in the previous chapter, it is a good idea to have some help in identifying your personality. This could be in the form of an online personality test, or by asking others who know you well to help you by describing you—just remember that their perception of you will be somewhat biased by their own relationship with you.

Your personality is important to your personal communications because it will affect how you see things, how you phrase things and how you react to others. It's well worth understanding yourself so that you can temper those words and reactions when you are discussing important issues. Understanding your own personality will also help you to understand why people view or judge you in the way that they do.

Many people feel that they treat others well, but that it's not reciprocated. Knowing your personality will help you to understand why this is, and to help change perceptions and build better relationships. There are many different personality types, according to the Myers-Briggs Type Indicator (MBTI, a self-assessment tool) 16 of them in all, and then many variations on those depending on each individual's strengths and weaknesses. What is important to know is that there is no right or wrong, and no good or bad personality. Everyone is different and experiences the world in different ways. Relationships are like a jigsaw puzzle with different 'shaped' relationships fitting together. By understanding this, you will be able to identify what areas of your relationship and communication need work, and which fall into place naturally.

Your Needs

Every person has needs. In a romantic relationship these needs are often very difficult to communicate in words, yet (consciously or subconsciously) we give signals all the time—some of which are read correctly, and some of which aren't. This miscommunication can cause trouble in an otherwise solid relationship. It is therefore important to identify, and how to express them. It goes without saying that we all need a roof over our heads, food on the table, clothes to wear, and probably some form of transport.

Emotional needs include things like trust. Do you feel that your partner trusts you? If not, think about why, and how you can make it easier for them to trust you. If you're a very independent and gregarious person you might unwittingly make it difficult for your partner to trust you by staying out late or not letting them know where you are. A quick message to let them know what you're up to and when you plan to be back could give them a sense of security.

Everybody yearns for some form of affection in their lives. Think about how you like affection to be shown. Are you a physical person? Does a hug or a hand squeeze satisfy that need, do you prefer to hear the words "I love you," do actions like receiving a gift, having someone hang paintings for you, or having your partner bring you coffee in bed best speak to your heart? While it's not your partner's duty to fulfil your every need, it would certainly help if they knew what it was that made you happy, so that they could express their affection in a way that works for both of you.

Space is another big factor. While connecting and doing things together as a couple is important, everybody needs a little space from time to time, and some people need a lot. This can also change according to what else is happening in your life. Perhaps you usually don't need much space, but you're battling with the death of a parent or a complicated work situation—then you may need more time alone for a while. Your partner however, doesn't have a crystal ball to consult, so you need to communicate your need for space to them. If you don't usually need much personal space, your partner could feel rejected by your sudden distancing, so it's important that you explain that it's not them you're avoiding, but that you rather need the time to deal with what you're going through and sort it out in your mind. Explain that this is temporary.

There are other emotional needs that you can consider in the same way, such as validation (proof that your partner admires you). You might need to receive compliments or maybe you just like your efforts to be recognized with a "thank you." Another one is empathy. How do you like your partner to show empathy? Some people want advice, but most really just want their feelings to be acknowledged, and again, this might change depending on the situation. If you communicate your needs to your partner in a gentle conversation, you can save yourself a confrontation that degenerates into criticisms and accusations.

Talk to your partner about your needs, if they know what makes you happy, the chances are that they will want to do exactly that, after all, they love you. Would you not love to have a "cheat sheet" on how to make your partner happy?

Know Your Partner

Strengths and Weaknesses

What are your partner's strengths and weaknesses? If you know these, and unless you share exactly the same strengths and weaknesses, this is where you can help each other out enormously. But unless you talk about it, and come up with a system that works for both of you, you could both end up very unhappy.

Perhaps your partner is a great cook, and in the interests of fair division of labor, you do the dishes. The only problem is your partner uses every utensil and dish in the kitchen and the place is a train smash when you arrive to clean up. You throw your hands in the air and say "can't you just make a little effort to not destroy the whole kitchen when you're cooking?"

Now your partner (who has put in a lot of effort to make you a delicious meal) feels completely unappreciated, and bites back with "well how about you do the cooking then?" Images of toast for dinner ratchet your annoyance up a level, and a big dispute is brewing.

By knowing your partner's strengths and weaknesses, you can choose how and when to broach the subject. For example, in this instance, time your discussion for when your partner has not just worked hard to make you happy, only to get criticized. Praise them for the lovely meal, and bite your tongue. Wait for a more opportune moment when they may be more receptive. If your partner has a good sense of humor, perhaps tease them and challenge them in a fun way, to use only five utensils and two pots or pans in the preparation of the next meal. Or if you know that Mondays are your worst day at work, and you usually come home tired and dreading the dishes, suggest that you get takeaways or do one dish wonders on a Monday. If you have home help once a week, suggest that the more complicated and creative dishes are prepared on that day.

However you go about resolving the problem of the messy kitchen, by understanding your partner's strengths and weaknesses, you will be able to make it a discussion rather than an argument. Keep to the facts: how to make the evening chores easier for both of you. Don't let it become about personal habits, who does more than the other, or what you like or don't like about each other. The problem is not in fact your partner, or you and your (apparent) lack of appreciation for their cooking; it is the amount of time spent on chores after work.

Personality

Having a good understanding of your partner's personality is key to deciding how and when to broach a subject, and key to making them happy. Having a happy partner also impacts your happiness enormously. When one partner in a relationship is miserable it doesn't take long for it to rub off on the other. The converse is also true though, so people who put thought and effort into making their partner happy, are ultimately ensuring a happy life for themselves.

Think about the personality traits that your partner has that originally attracted you to them, make a list of these. Then, make a list of their personality traits that make you feel unhappy. When you are communicating with them, use this understanding of their personality to shape your conversation.

Let's say that your partner is a confident person and someone who likes to help people by solving problems. Confidence is a very attractive quality, and so is caring (the reason why your partner likes to solve problems for others). Now, perhaps you have a problem with your boss at work that's getting you down. You need to share the problem, but you don't want to be told what to do, you just want a sympathetic ear. Knowing your partner's personality, you will suspect that they will be inclined to want to phone the boss or give you advice on how you should be dealing with it; so you'd rather just stew about it by yourself. You then start wishing you had someone to share your problem with, but, discount your partner as a possibility.

This is not fair on your partner. Yes, they may be naturally inclined to give advice, but this is not because they're 'controlling' or 'interfering,' it's because they care and want to help. Try saying to your partner, "I've got a work issue that is worrying me, and I want to talk about it, but I'm feeling a bit sensitive and I really want to be able to solve it myself. I'd like to talk to you just so that you can understand what I'm going through, and to help me understand it myself, but I don't want any advice." You may well be surprised to find that your partner is happy to oblige, knowing what it is that they can do to show their care and will be sympathetic without trying to solve it.

Likewise, knowing that your partner is caring can help you to make your partner happy by understanding their need to express that care. When your partner is always heading off to help someone in distress, you might feel abandoned and unloved. Instead of accusing them of caring more about everyone else than they do about you, say "I've been missing you lately, let's do something together this weekend."

Their Needs

Your partner's needs will undoubtedly be based on the same major categories that yours are. However, they may be very different.

We discussed trust in relation to your needs. Your partner also needs to be trusted, and conversely, to be able to trust you. By communicating where you are going and when you think you'll be home, or sending a text if you're running late, you gain that trust for yourself, and help your partner to feel secure. Perhaps because you're such an independent person, you might find your partner's insecurities a bit odd and even stifling.

By understanding that your partner needs to feel secure rather than controlling, you will be open to sharing more openly. It's easy for you to know what your needs are, but you can only guess at what your partners needs are, unless they are communicated clearly. In the absence of absolute certainty, the best thing to do is *ask*. Guesswork, is assuming, and as mentioned previously, assumption is the cause of most communication breakdowns.

So, if your partner keeps asking where you were, and what you were doing, this should tell you something. If it doesn't, then ask. Don't get defensive or angry because you assume that it's because they don't trust you. Rather ask, "why do you worry when I'm not home on time, and what can I do to reduce your concerns?" You might be surprised to find that their concern is about what time to start dinner so that it's freshly cooked when you get home and has nothing to do with trust at all, or you might find that your partner has been cheated on in a previous relationship, or you have been too busy and distracted by work lately, and they just need some reassurance that they still matter.

Don't assume that you know your partner's needs. You can learn a lot by observing their behavior, but every time you are uncertain, ask. Needs change with age and with changing circumstances, so even what you used to know in respect of their needs may not be the same. A sure sign that someone's needs are not being met is when tension develops in a relationship. Don't go on the attack, "What's the matter with you?" is usually responded to by an abrupt "nothing," and we all know that means "everything!" Be genuinely interested, and say something like, "I'm sensing that something is worrying you, is there anything I can do to make it better?"

Understand How This Knowledge Impacts Communication

Once you know yourself and your partner, and understand each other's beliefs and values you can use this knowledge to ensure that you communicate effectively.

You do this by considering what upsets or motivates you and likewise, your partner. Avoid saying or doing things that are going to trigger unhappiness or defensiveness, and focus your discussion on things that will be positively received. These are valuable tools for ensuring that your discussion results in finding common ground rather than causing upset.

For instance, your partner might not pick up on hints very well. In this case it's pointless sighing and huffing and puffing while trying to open a jar in the hope that they will come to your aid. Rather, take the jar to them and ask them if they could open it for you. They will probably be happy to do something to help, and glad that you asked. Whereas, if you keep trying without asking, you might become resentful and think that they don't care about you because they're leaving you to struggle. And they may be quite hurt if you suddenly lash out at them about being unhelpful.

Some people find it difficult to ask for help. If you know that you find it difficult to do so, you will also know that it's something that you need to work on, and practice being more direct with your partner.

Be careful of assuming that you know your partner too well though. If they give a response that is hurtful, critical or negative, don't assume the worst. Tell them gently how it makes you feel, and why, and ask them if you're reading too much into it. This will often diffuse a potentially negative situation.

Chapter 3

Planning to Send

Decide on What Type of Communication is Best Suited to the Situation

Every situation is different, and you need to decide what form of communication will work best for you. Some situations call for one on one discussions, either telephonically or in person, while others are better communicated in a group situation, or by email or letter. Below we look at these options and which are best suited to what situations.

Sometimes in conflict situations a letter is best, especially if you have tried to discuss the matter previously, but failed because it always seems to degenerate into a row. This is also the case when what you have to say is important and detailed and you believe your audience is likely to interrupt you.

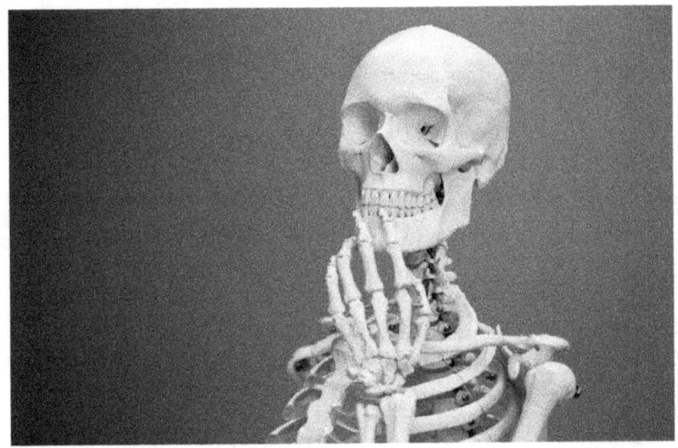

Face to Face

Face to face communication is probably the most commonly experienced. You use it naturally in everyday situations, at the supermarket, in social situations, in romantic situations, and at work. It is also often the most successful, as your message is relayed not only by the words you use, but by your facial expressions, body language, and tone of voice. Imagine that you need to tell someone that they've made a mistake, but you don't want to upset them in turn—your message will be reinforced non-verbally if you are sitting with your arms at your sides and that you are looking at them with a sympathetic smile.

Face to face communication is best in the following situations:

- If you are going to break news to someone that may shock or upset them. You want to be there to support them with a hug or sugar water for shock, and you want to be sure that they are in a safe space to receive this information, not driving along the highway. It would be callous to send someone a text telling them that a close family member has passed away.
- If you want to stress the importance of the message that you are giving them, and their importance to you. For instance, if you were asking someone to marry you, or disciplining an employee for a serious transgression. If distance is not an issue, these would be better done in person rather than on the telephone or via a letter or email.
- If you need to discuss a sensitive situation. Being face to face will give you additional clues as to how the person or people you are talking to are reacting to the discussion, and will help you to adjust your approach or your tone accordingly. When raising a sensitive issue with a person, doing so face to face, behind closed doors is best, as they will feel more secure and be likely to be more open with you.

In Writing

Writing is most commonly used for business purposes, and less so for personal, especially in modern times, when video chats via the internet are so easily accessible.

However, there is still a time and place for written communications in most situations:

- When you want to provide a lot of detail. It's best to do it writing, even if you go through it in person and use the written 'manual' as a hand out. This will help you to put your thoughts in the right order, make sure you're not leaving anything out, and provide your audience with something that they can refer back to.

- When you think that there's trouble brewing at work or in business. If you think that a situation is likely to end up in a disciplinary hearing, or in court, where it can boil down to "he said vs. she said," then it's best to have a paper trail or proof. This is where email comes into its own. While you may not record a conversation without the consent of both parties, you can communicate via email for a precise record.

- If you're placing an order for something, or booking accommodation or a paid service, email again ensures that there is proof of what you ordered, and what was agreed to. Basically any communication around a transaction should have some record that you can refer back to if things should go wrong.

- Sometimes written communication can be very valuable in a romantic or personal relationship too. If you are dealing with a conflict or emotionally charged situation where both parties get heated and defensive, it can sometimes be difficult to make your point verbally without being interrupted or having the person you're communicating with getting defensive and not listening to what you're saying. When a person is feeling attacked, they get defensive, and are too busy trying to work out their response to be able to give your message their undivided attention. Even you might get too upset to be able to remember all the important points you need to explain to them in order to get them to understand your point of view. This is where having the time to word your message carefully and avoiding interruptions or hysterical outbursts is very useful.

One on One

Both in the workplace and socially, one on one communication is very important if you need to criticize and/or correct another person, or raise a sensitive issue.

Let's be honest, nobody likes criticism, but to criticize or correct someone in front of their colleagues or friends is humiliating for the recipient. Not only will they feel belittled, they will not accept the criticism well. They are not likely to thank you and promise to do better, they are going to go into defensive mode.

Criticizing your partner or pointing out their faults publicly will never earn you any sympathy. It will be perceived by others present as bullying—even if your partner is in the wrong, they will be likely to have the support of the audience. Nobody likes to watch someone else being bullied.

Sometimes gender may also be a reason for a one on one conversation. You wouldn't, as the only female in an office or even one of a minority, want the boss to discuss with you the clogging of the office toilet with sanitary towels in front of everyone.

Group Address

There are times when addressing a group is obvious, for instance, if you are making a speech at an event or conference. There are other occasions when addressing a group is a good idea, these include:

- If you're announcing a change in procedure or company ownership. You won't have time to sit down and explain it to every employee, but if it's important, you also don't just want to send a letter. In these circumstances, speaking to them as a group, and allowing for a question and answer session afterwards is best.

- You may also want to recognize certain people for their achievements. They will appreciate public recognition either instead of, or in addition to a personal congratulations.

- If staff morale has been low, it is worthwhile addressing them together, showing that you understand their feelings and getting their input into how to build a happier, more productive team.

- If a situation involves a number of family members, discussing it as a group may save some people from feeling that they have been left out or their opinions are being overlooked. Or, worse, wondering what you've been saying behind their backs.

Adapting Your Communication Style to your Audience

We discussed in chapters one and two how important it is to know not only yourself, but the person (or people) you will be communicating with. Here, we take a more in-depth look at how to put this knowledge into practice when planning what you're going to say, and how you should say it.

Let's first take a look at planning what you're going to say. Consider your audience, and the message you are needing to get across to them. The first step to planning this, is to think about who you are going to be addressing. Sometimes the same message needs to be passed on to more than one person, but the content needs to be changed according to who you are talking to, and what you want from that person.

In this first example, imagine that you are in a financially difficult situation, the company you work for is downsizing and you are being let go. You are renting a nice big house with a swimming pool, and will no longer be able to afford the rent.

You would need to give your partner as much information as possible, so that you can work together on a way forward and plan new budgets. Your partner will need to know details such as how much your severance pay will be, whether you qualify for any government assistance, and what your short-term job prospects look like. You may want sympathy and even financial support from your partner.

When it comes to telling your child however, too much information could overwhelm them and erode their sense of security. Children don't have the coping mechanisms to deal with adult problems and should not be burdened with them. You only need to tell your child that you are not going to be working for a while, that you will be moving and will have to do without a few luxuries for a few months, but that it is a temporary situation. You would want to allay their fears and give the impression that things are under control.

You would want your young child to accept that things have changed, but have them still feel loved and secure. You may want to emphasize that while you may be living in a different house, they will still be going to the same school, or if that isn't possible, that they will be going to a new school, but their old school friends will still be welcome to visit. You may appeal to their sense of adventure and focus on the positives of the new school or house.

Now let's look at a work situation using the Covid-19 pandemic of 2020. Your company has had to change the way they do things. New protocols have to be implemented, and it's your job to get everyone on board. The boss is going to need to know how much all the equipment is going to cost, and how your new protocols align with industry standards as well as how and when training will take place etc. The rest of the staff don't need that much information, and too much information could leave them feeling overwhelmed and detract from what's important to them.

In this case, you would provide the boss with a full, detailed, written report, and then provide a summary of the bottom line in terms of how it will affect working hours, what it will cost and what industry guidelines were used to formulate the plan. The rest of the employees would be best divided into groups according to their duties, and provided with the information necessary to them. Let's say you work for a hotel. You would segment the employees into departments, as each department would have its own set of protocols e.g. kitchen, food and beverage service staff, housekeeping, bellhops, maintenance, etc. This way you could plan your presentation around duties that are specific to them.

Make Them Feel Comfortable

By planning separate communication sessions for different departments as in the above example, you will be able to leave out unnecessary information that may detract from their focus, and keep it relevant. While the big picture is good for everyone, this can be summarized. Food and beverage servers will need to know about how the new protocols affect them, and you could lose their attention if you discussed sanitizing luggage, or bedrooms. So, keep it focused and relevant. They need to know about what happens at the bar and in the restaurant. What has changed in *their* daily routines and how *they* need to adapt. By separating the groups, you can also use relevant examples that they can connect with.

You will be able to "use their language." Some terms are familiar to service staff, but not to others, e.g. appetizer, or serving station. You can hone in on examples that your audience relates to. Staying with the waiters, you can describe a situation where a guest sends their plate of food back to the kitchen because their steak is under-done, and how to handle the plate in a manner that avoids any potential contamination.

By knowing your audience, what motivates them, and what frustrations they experience, you can not only make your message more relevant, but get them on your side. You can express sympathy for them if they have to battle to make themselves heard through a face mask that muffles voices, or dealing with the heat of the kitchen under a face mask in summer time. You can show consideration for their discomfort by providing hand cream to help with the drying effect of constantly hand sanitizing—or if the boss won't buy it for them, suggest that they bring their own. Just knowing that you are aware of and care about their discomfort will help them to feel appreciated.

Making your audience feel comfortable is not only about group addresses, and using examples that are familiar to them. It is also about creating a safe environment where they feel that they can be honest without being judged or fearing reprisals. If the person you are speaking to feels that they can be honest with you and that you will listen to and consider their point of view, you are likely to get to the bottom of the matter and find solutions to problems far more quickly than if they are feeling defensive and weighing up their words carefully to avoid retaliation.

A safe environment can be the physical environment, the actual place where the discussion takes place. Imagine that you are concerned about a rumor that your spouse is having an affair. At this stage, you don't know for sure if they are or not, and you want to find out if it's true. This is likely to be a difficult conversation for your spouse. The chances are that they will either be defensive and angry at being caught out, or terribly disappointed that you could even think such a thing. Either way, it's going to provoke an emotional response. Put yourself in their shoes and think about how you would react to such an 'accusation.' This is a very private matter, so, don't bring it up over dinner in a restaurant, or any public place for that matter.

Have you ever had an emotional discussion in a car? Where tempers rise, there are tears and recriminations, and you feel trapped because you can't walk away or take time out? Both of you should be able to take time out if necessary, even if it's just going to the bathroom to blow your nose or splash water on your face. So, choose your physical space with care.

A safe environment is also a "mental space." You need to create a non-judgmental mood. Don't work on assumptions. Work with facts, and let the person you're talking to know that you are listening to them and not being aggressive. Tell them that you trust them and want to hear their version of events, don't make an accusation without having done this. In the previous example, you might start your conversation with "I heard a disturbing rumor the other day, and am hoping that you can set it right for me…"

The same applies in a work situation. If you dive in with an accusation based on something you've heard, the person you're talking to will automatically assume that you have already judged them, and that you are on the side of the person who told you, not theirs. This will make them defensive and they will either be belligerent or defensive—or both. They may even lie to cover up because they're afraid of the consequences. However, if you take a neutral stance, and show genuine interest in their version of events, they are far more likely to open up and share information, be willing to take advice, and even help you to solve the problem.

Timing is also an important part of creating a safe space. Don't tackle serious or potentially emotional issues with your spouse immediately after a special or romantic moment, or at a time when they are feeling vulnerable. This will detract from what you have just shared, and your partner may think that the connection they felt with you was one-sided because you were not connecting, you were busy "planning an attack."

The same theory applies at work. If someone has just received an award or sealed a great deal, now is not the time to talk to them about their lack of punctuality. Recognize their achievement, congratulate them, and let them enjoy the moment. File your discussion on punctuality for a more opportune moment. If you say "well done, that's a fantastic achievement, but imagine how much better you could do if you actually came to work on time…" you are diminishing their achievement, and your support of them. Don't spoil the moment. Rather, wait a day or two, and then broach the subject. When you do discuss it, unless the person is a repeat offender who has been warned numerous times, let them know that you are looking at it as a problem that needs to be resolved, rather than an attack on them. Ask, "I've noticed that you are struggling to get to work on time in the mornings, what is the issue behind it?" This is going to make them far more open to jointly solving the problem than "why are you late again?"

People genuinely do want peace in their lives, and it's never wise to just assume the worst. They may have a very good reason, and be more than willing to change if you show concern for them rather than criticism. Maybe your colleague who is always late has to leave home early and catch a bus to work because they don't have a car. Perhaps they live on the same route as another colleague, and would be happy to chip in for fuel and get a lift to work. By creating a safe environment for this discussion and approaching it from a neutral or even supportive stance, you will be able to get to the heart of the matter without unnecessary drama.

It's important that you adapt your communication style to suit the needs of your audience. Use terms that they are familiar with, examples that they understand, and even body language and gestures that they can associate with. The more 'real' and relatable you come across to your audience and the safer they feel in a discussion with you, the better your chances are of achieving the goal of your communication. Remember earlier we touched on considering *why* you are communicating with a specific person or group, and what you want from them as a result of this communication. This is where it all starts to fall into place.

Chapter 4:

Sending

Communication Styles

It's all very well, talking about how to communicate best in different situations, but nobody expects you to "fake it" all the time! Everybody has their own default style of communication. If you Google communication styles, you will discover that these are largely divided into four categories. Passive, Aggressive, Passive-Aggressive, and Assertive. We will discuss these in detail in this chapter. Think about which one sounds most like you.

Your default communication style is the one that comes naturally, or is most obvious, when you are involved in an unplanned, heated conversation (or disagreement). Being aware of your default communication style, and that of your audience, is very helpful when planning an important discussion. It will help you to curb your natural tendencies that might be counterproductive to your goals, and help you to understand and deal with issues that could arise based on the personality and communication style of the person you're communicating with.

Mary Clare Novak, a content marketing specialist with a focus on customer relationship management, describes the effect of this well in her blog, *4 Types of Communications Styles*, and which one is most effective when she compares it to styles of clothing and the impression this makes:

"The way we dress says a lot about us.

It might seem artificial, but we make assumptions about people based on what they are currently wearing. If you saw someone in a freshly pressed suit you would assume they were headed to an important business meeting, and if you saw someone in a bathing suit and flip flops, you would point them in the direction of the nearest beach.

The same goes for the way we communicate. When we adopt a certain style of communication, it implies certain things about our personality, mood, and even the type of conversation you are having.

Each individual's personal style can be completely unique, but they still typically fall into a certain category: grunge, chic, hipster, professional. This is also the case for our communication styles." (Novak, 2019.)

What this means for you as a communicator is that you create a certain impression by the way that you communicate, and that you can anticipate certain reactions, or at the very least, understand the reactions of the person you are communicating with.

As you read through the different styles below, think about who they remind you of.

Passive

Passive communicators generally like to think of themselves as 'non-confrontational,' they will hold back on giving their opinion or avoid conflict situations. While this seems to be a good thing, it can cause more harm than you would think. It's not only damaging to their confidence, and prevents them from being an active participant in resolving issues, but can result in an unhealthy buildup of resentment that eventually erupts and could completely blindside the other party, who is blissfully unaware of the pending storm.

Some signs of a passive communicator include:

- Poor posture, slouching, and not looking you in the eye
- They are not confident and don't want to rock the boat

- They rarely venture an opinion, preferring to agree with everyone or just keep quiet
- They rarely take risks or come up with new ideas
- They procrastinate and are indecisive
- They apologize even when it's not their fault
- They have low self-esteem

They are inclined to say things like:

- "Nobody cares what I feel"
- "My opinion doesn't count"
- "I get taken advantage of"
- "I can't do anything about it"
- "I'm probably wrong"

One of the biggest problems experienced by passive communicators is that they don't want to draw attention to themselves and are afraid to express an opinion. This means that they withdraw from communicating effectively. Instead of solving problems through clear communication, they send mixed signals. They are inclined to say "I don't mind," rather than stipulating what their preference is. When in fact they may mind very much, but just can't bring themselves to say so.

This suppression of their true feelings leads to discontent, and they may start to feel victimized and even start irritating others because they always act hard-done by. They become martyrs of their own making.

If you are a passive communicator, you need to realize that by not asserting yourself, sharing your opinions and giving people clear signals as to what you like and don't like, or what you need from them, you are doing both yourself and the other person a disservice. You are preventing yourself from being heard, and constantly subjecting yourself to the will of others. At the same time, you are not allowing others the opportunity to make your life easier and happier.

You might think that you're just being nice and easy going, but you're actually causing issues by not addressing them and giving all the wrong signals. This can even be the result of just trying to "be nice." I once heard a story of a young man, who on meeting his prospective mother-in-law for the first time, was served sheep brains for dinner. It made him feel quite queasy, but trying to please his fiancé's mother, he soldiered on until his plate was clean, and raved about how delicious it was. He eventually got married, and his mother-in-law, a very caring lady, as a special treat, would serve sheep brains every time he visited!

If you know that you are going to be dealing with a passive communicator, help them to be heard. Encourage them to share their opinions by saying things like, "I know you don't mind, but what would make you happy? Your feelings are important to me."

Aggressive

Aggressive communicators take self confidence to the next level. They are often gossiped about behind their backs because they talk about me, myself, and I. They are inclined to pay little attention to the rights of others.

While self-confidence is a good thing, and being opinionated and unafraid to share these opinions may initially impress people and see you climbing the ladder (either socially or at work), it's very hard to live with an aggressive communicator, and more often than not, they don't make good leaders.

They eventually step on everyone's toes and leave behind a trail of hurt feelings and resentment. While they feel that they are being strong, getting things done, and even amusing others, they are often completely unaware of the fact that they are coming across as brash, egotistical, and full of swagger.

Here are some signs to look out for:

- they speak loudly and demand attention

- they have an opinion on everything
- they dominate conversations
- they use sarcasm frequently
- they're inclined to interrupt others
- they are critical of others
- they are more inclined toward apportioning blame than finding solutions
- they are not good listeners
- they are not shy about extolling their virtues
- everything is always somebody else's fault
- they are likely to criticize or belittle you in public
- they show little or no regard for the feelings or rights of others

They are inclined to say things like:

- "I know what I'm talking about"
- "of course I'm right"
- "I don't take things lying down"
- "It's my way or the highway"
- "you don't have to like it"
- "It's your fault"
- "because I said so..."

Not pleasant, right? Surprisingly, a lot of aggressive communicators are not aware that they are being overbearing and making others uncomfortable. They think of themselves as being strong, leading the troops, and making things happen.

Others see them condescending, ungrateful, full of themselves, and very often just downright rude. They don't inspire people to do their best, they dominate them and force them to do their best out of fear of the consequences. At first, they may have success, as fear sets in, but eventually lose this advantage as they lose the respect of those around them, and people stop seeking their opinions and even start avoiding them, or removing themselves from their sphere of influence.

Do you recognize some of the aggressive communicator's sayings? Do you describe yourself as an alpha personality? Maybe you're frustrated by the incompetence that surrounds you? If you do, be careful. Others may think that you're victimizing them—even when you don't mean to.

If the person you are planning a communication with has an aggressive communication style, you'll need to work extra hard at creating a soothing atmosphere. Provide something to eat or drink, most people are at their most relaxed after a meal or a drink. No wonder so many business deals revolve around a lunch, a cup of coffee, or a beer!

Know that the person is likely to interrupt you, and keep a list of the main points you wanted to cover so that you can check that you haven't been railroaded into forgetting what you wanted to communicate. Be prepared to stand up for your point of view, without getting sucked into an argument or screaming match. The best way to do this is to prepare yourself mentally beforehand, and if the person you are communicating with becomes angry or emotional, remind yourself "I will not raise my voice, I will not get angry."

A trick that works quite well when going into a potentially explosive work situation, is to tell yourself that you are playing a role, that nothing that's about to transpire has anything to do with you or your feelings. Tell yourself that you are simply playing the role of a supporting and understanding colleague/boss/subordinate, and it is the other person's job to try and get you to lose your cool. You win if you don't get sucked into the drama.

I have emphasized a work situation in the scenario above, because while this works well to protect you from work aggression; it can exacerbate aggression in a close personal situation where the person you're communicating with may be encouraged to try harder to get an emotional reaction out of you.

In a romantic relationship, or a close family one, you can protect yourself by telling yourself that they don't mean the hurtful things they are saying. It's best to deal with small things in a casual manner than to let issues blow out of proportion, and very likely professional help may be needed in order to get your loved one to recognize how hurtful their behavior can be, and to encourage change.

Passive-Aggressive

The passive-aggressive style of communication is the least successful. It is confusing. Passive-Aggressives are inconsistent and difficult to read. As unpleasant as an aggressive communicator is, at least you know where you stand with them!

A passive-aggressive person not only makes those around them miserable, they make themselves miserable too. They estrange the people they care about through their behavior, yet still feel that they are the victims.

Many passive-aggressive communicators honestly think that by hiding their aggression, they are avoiding conflict. What they don't realize is that they aren't hiding their aggression at all, they're actually just delivering it in a sneakier way, and making matters worse. Because they're incapable of saying what they mean and standing by it, they feel ineffective, and start to develop resentment toward the person they feel is responsible for their unhappiness.

Some signs of a passive-aggressive communicator include:

- Inconsistent body language e.g. saying something nasty with a smile, or something that sounds like it could be a compliment, but with a sarcastic tone or a frown "e.g. well aren't you clever…"
- When there's clearly something upsetting them, but they won't admit to it, because they don't want to face it.
- They don't take you on if you challenge or criticize them, but mutter behind your back as you leave the room.
- Their words and actions don't gel. They might say that they support your idea, but then do things to prevent it from becoming a reality.

- Sighing, sulking, or eye rolling.
- Not greeting you or acknowledging you.
- Instead of saying no to a request you make, they do it, but with bad grace.
- Dropping hints instead of telling you what they really feel.

They are inclined to say things like:

- "whatever!"
- "oh, I thought you knew"
- "what's the big rush?"
- backhanded compliments like, "I love your haircut, it makes you look more mature"
- "I'm not upset"
- "I wish *I* could…" (fill in the blank with whatever springs to mind) "But that's never going to happen"
- "I'm only telling you this because I care about you…" (then proceed to insult you)
- "I know this is probably going to upset you, but…"

If you recognize yourself in the descriptions above, it's time to take a long hard look at your communication style. You'll definitely get a more positive response from people if you tell them what is worrying you. Deal with issues as they arise, don't let them become huge obstacles to your happiness. Stop trying to give people clues as to your unhappiness, they won't be able to guess it right every time, and will eventually get tired of trying to.

If you recognize the person you are going to be addressing then, steel yourself. You are going to have to be alert to all the other signals, body language, facial expressions, and little huffs and puffs. You're also going to need to draw the truth out of them. Say things like, "I want to help you but I don't know what you want," or "Let's just play open cards, it's going to be so much easier to find common ground if we're upfront about how we're feeling."

The best thing you can do for a passive-aggressive person if you need to deal with a sensitive issue, is create a safe space where they are not feeling judged, attacked, or defensive. Try to start your conversation with a positive, and then create empathy by relating to how they must be feeling. If you can, tell a story that puts you in a similar position at some stage and how you felt in that situation. Let them know that you are able to be objective and view things from their perspective too, but ask them to help you to do this.

Assertive

Assertive communication is not the same as aggressive communication. It is diplomatic and considers the feelings and rights of others as well as yourself. It is the most effective of all the communication styles both at work and at home, because it is open, honest, and considerate.

Being assertive involves expressing your needs and wants, rather than suppressing them in favor of others. It makes it much easier for others to understand you and give you what you want. It is not however, a manipulative way of communicating. It doesn't put your needs ahead of others, it involves weighing up both parties needs and finding solutions that are mutually beneficial. If it's not your default style, don't stress, it can be learned and perfected through practice.

Some signs of an assertive communicator are:

- relaxed body language (upright with arms at the sides)
- looking the other person in the eye
- listening
- clearly expressing needs and wants
- using 'I' statements rather than 'you'
- Being respectful
- Being honest
- Speaking calmly

They are inclined to say things like:

- "help me understand why…"
- "I can't do it now, but let's talk in an hour's time"
- "you're right, that's something I need to work on"
- "I hear what you're saying, but here's why I don't agree"
- "it would be a great help to me if you…"
- "why do you feel that way?"
- "I'd love to help you, but today's not good for me, how would tomorrow suit you?"
- "I was worried when you didn't respond to my message"
- "I get overwhelmed when I don't have help with the housework"
- "I know you're under pressure from the client, but I need a bit more time for big projects so that I can plan properly and get it right. Can we negotiate a longer period?"

Being assertive is about being honest, without being disrespectful or invalidating others' feelings. It makes other people feel comfortable because they know where they stand with you, what you need or expect of them, and that you care about their needs. It's about not being afraid of the other person's reaction, and understanding that there will be times when no matter how polite or diplomatic you are, others might take offense or respond badly, but that you aren't responsible for their feelings, and are open to hearing them out and resolving matters and compromising to restore harmony.

Having said that, there is no single communication style that suits every situation. There are times when it is necessary to be aggressive, or even passive. If the building was on fire, and your colleague was looking for her handbag before leaving, you would be justified in barking out instructions instead of negotiating. Likewise, there are times when you might just have to suppress your needs for a while if someone else is going through a traumatic or difficult time, and needs your support, even if it's not convenient. It's not about who is more important, but rather whose needs are more urgent at that specific time. It's about prioritizing.

Under normal circumstances, assertive communication is very good for relationship building because it provides both parties with a clear understanding of each other's needs. People feel more confident and secure when they know what is expected of them, and it helps to prevent private resentments, ongoing awkwardness, or fear of failure. Think of the poor chap who endured the 'treat' of sheep brains for the rest of his married life. If only, instead of enthusing, he had said "I'm not sure if I'll ever get past my mental block about eating offal, but I must say it's better than I thought it would be. You must be a great cook."

Chapter 5:

Receiving

Now that you have planned on what message you want to send, who you are going to be communicating with, and what you want from them, it's time to focus on the second part of communication. Remember it's a two-way street, involving both sending and receiving, writing and reading, or speaking and listening.

Just talking is not communicating. It might be better described as lecturing. For effective communication you need to be able to get feedback, take it on board and if necessary, explain for better clarity or adjust your approach to get support.

Receiving involves more than just hearing. Hearing and listening are commonly confused. Hearing is when your ear notices a sound, listening involves much more than that, it entails engaging with the sound. To listen, you concentrate on the words and their meaning. Sometimes though, the words that are *not* spoken can tell you much more than what was actually said, and there are other cues like body language, tone of voice, etc. that will help give you a clearer picture. To communicate effectively, you need to involve your ears, your eyes, and your brain. You need to have some understanding of your audience to put what they're saying into context.

Receiving With Your Ears

Focusing on the Speaker

Have you ever heard an adult say to their child "Look at me when I'm talking to you"? Ever wished you could say that to your boss? It's very frustrating trying to have a conversation with your husband when he's watching sports on the TV, or trying to pitch an important idea to your boss, who is constantly looking at their watch or responding to texts on their phone. You feel angry because they are just not giving you their undivided attention, you feel you're wasting your time.

That's how your audience will feel if you don't focus on them. In order for communication to be effective, both parties must be committed to the process. So, when you are receiving, give it your all. Focus on the person that is speaking. Face them, make eye contact. Don't stare them down, keep it relaxed. You can look away from time to time, that's natural, but don't stare out of the window or look at your computer screen. Focus on what they are saying, and don't interrupt them to get your point of view across, let them finish what they are saying before you respond.

Don't daydream, answer telephone calls, try and guess what's coming next, or plan your response while they are speaking, take in what they are saying, and think about it in context. In a work situation, taking notes is a great way to keep yourself focused and on track. Listen to their tone of voice, do they sound upbeat, depressed, excited, nervous? This helps to put what they're saying in context. Also, listen to what they're *not* saying—in other words, read between the lines. Don't get carried away with assumptions, just be aware of signs of hesitance or resistance.

Some people are not comfortable expressing their disagreement (remember the passive and passive-aggressive communicators?). Just because somebody didn't oppose your idea or plan, doesn't mean they support it. If you say to your family, "let's go to an Italian restaurant for dinner tonight" and the response is, "we could…" it sounds positive, but actually, there is hesitation there. What aren't they telling you? Maybe they have other plans but don't want to hurt your feelings, or maybe they are keen to go out, but would prefer Chinese or Mexican food. Perhaps ordering in from different restaurants would be a better option.

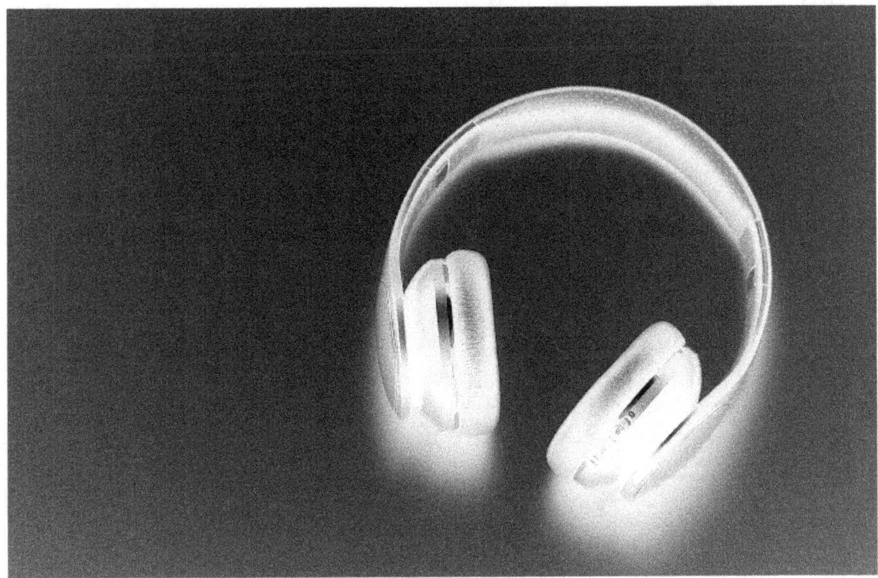

Avoiding Interruptions

Only in an ideal world can you sit down and have a discussion without any interruptions whatsoever. Life happens around you. The phone rings, the dog barks, someone knocks at the door, or you knock your cup of coffee over on your desk. These are unplanned. However, when holding an important conversation these can be minimized. Ask the switchboard to hold your calls, switch your mobile off, and make an effort to stay focused.

If there is an interruption, ask the person speaking to you to hold that thought, deal with it quickly, and return your attention to them. Don't launch forth with what's on your mind when you do. Remember that they were speaking, and encourage them to continue. If you can, you should also "hold that thought" so that you can restart the conversation by showing them that you were listening, say "you were telling me about…"

If you are sitting around the boardroom table and someone is making a point when they are interrupted by another participant, if you allow the interruption, the chances are strong that you will make the first speaker feel that you don't value their opinion, or that you value the interruptor's opinion more. It would be preferable in a situation like this to say to the person who is interrupting "Hang on a second, I just want to hear the end of what X is saying, then I'm keen to get your opinion."

Show Encouragement

In order to have a successful team in the workplace, it's necessary to encourage your employees to share their opinions and challenges.

You can do this by having an open-door policy, letting employees know that you are aware of them, and the difficulties that they might be experiencing with their work. You make yourself available to listen and advise them. Many companies claim to have open communication policies, but fail dismally at actually implementing them. Usually because the boss is too busy, or thinks they're too important to be wasting time on the employees with (in their eyes) relatively minor, problems.

This is a big mistake and can sabotage teamwork terribly. The employee who feels comfortable approaching their boss with an issue is confident in sharing their opinion, pointing out when things aren't working, and can help the boss steer the team to success. It can be difficult to always make time, but it's definitely worth doing.

If an employee comes to you with a problem, give them your undivided attention. Sit forward and focus on them. Keep your posture relaxed and don't keep looking at the time. Don't be critical. Appreciate the fact that it took your employee courage to approach you, and tell them that you value their opinion.

Don't always wait for them to volunteer an opinion, ask them for their thoughts and whether they have concerns when starting a new project. Get regular updates from them—this will help you to detect problems before they become serious. A quick "how are you doing?" goes a long way.

Many of your employees will also have useful suggestions. They usually work directly with the company's clients and experience their frustrations and suggestions. They are a rich source of information on what your customers want, what they like, and what they don't.

The simplest way of making your employees feel valued is to just greet them. Give them a smile and make them feel welcome when they arrive, and wish them a good evening when you or they leave. You don't have to visit them at home on the weekends, but make them feel part of the 'family' by acknowledging the fact that they have families, problems, and celebrations outside of the workplace.

Celebrate birthdays, and commiserate if they are experiencing a loss or going through a divorce. Thank them for their opinions, and congratulate them when they've done a good job. Just by being human, and acknowledging that they are more than a machine, you will create a culture of caring. This caring in turn will earn you their loyalty, but give them the sense of security that is so important to honest communication.

When employees feel heard and appreciated, they will be happier to own up to mistakes and become part of the solution rather than the problem, and not covering things up until you find yourself with an unmitigated disaster on your hands.

In a romantic relationship, your partner should also feel that they can tell you anything. It will only help you to have a better relationship. Whether they're concerned about finances, awkward about sex, or feeling insecure—all of those concenrs can be allayed just by being non-judgmental when they do share with you. If you sense tension in your partner, ask, they're probably desperate to discuss something with you but afraid of your reaction.

Clarify If You're Not Sure

Sometimes you can pick up on stress even when it hasn't been verbalized. Clarify if you're not sure. It's the simplest thing to ask someone if you're reading them correctly. Sometimes you get mixed signals, and you may well end up doing something you hate, like sitting through a two-hour ballet, just because you *think* it's what will make your partner happy, only to find out later that you were both dreading it. This is especially true in the early years of a romance when you don't know each other well.

At work when you are given a job, if you are not absolutely certain how the boss wants it done, ask. There is nothing worse than working really hard on a project only to have to redo it all because you missed the brief. Even if you have the slightest doubt, you can be sure that the boss would be far happier if you 'wasted' five minutes of their time on what to you may seem "trivial details," and get a well turned out project on the deadline than presented something that completely missed the mark and needs to be redone at the last minute.

The same applies to duties. There is a very good reason that companies have job descriptions. If you have an outline that tells you exactly what is your responsibility and what is not, you are unlikely to get in trouble for not doing something that someone else expected of you. Think about a meeting, where the boss says, "will someone please take the minutes." You start writing, but then look up and see another colleague also writing, so you stop, thinking that there's no point in you both doing it.

You get to the end of the meeting and the boss asks you, specifically, to have the minutes typed up and sent out. You look to your colleague and say, "weren't you taking the minutes?" They shake their head, "no, I was just doodling, the boss looked at you when he asked." Now you're in trouble, and all because you didn't check.

If taking minutes was not part of your regular job description, when you noticed your colleague writing, you should have clarified who was taking the minutes.

Receiving With Your Eyes

An effective communicator doesn't only listen with their ears, they use their eyes to tell them whether they are interpreting the message they are receiving correctly. This is referred to as body language, something that will be discussed in greater detail in Chapter 7 because while it is a way of reinforcing a message, it can also contradict the message, making it a barrier to communication.

Be Aware of Cultural Differences

Be alert when communicating with people of a different culture, that what you may deem to be polite, respectful, or friendly, they may not. In some cultures, it is rude to be too punctual. Arriving bang on time could earn you a frown from your hostess who will feel rushed. So, don't rush to chide your employee or friend for their tardiness if you don't know their culture.

In a number of European and Eastern countries, it is impolite to enter the house with your shoes on. You need to remove them at the door, and enter in slippers or barefoot, so choose your outfit accordingly. While in other countries, belching after a meal is considered a compliment to the host or hostess, though depending on your source this unusual trait might just be a myth.

This can extend beyond simple etiquette, into the realm of communication. If you were talking to a Brazilian and they were nodding from time to time, you may be forgiven for thinking that they are in agreement with you. However, you would be wrong. Brazilians nod their heads (up and down) to indicate "no," and shake them from side to side to indicate "yes"—the complete opposite of the USA and Britain.

A thumbs up is seen in most western countries as a sign of something positive, whether it's a greeting, or a quick "okay." Try it in a country like Greece and you may find you're unwittingly courting trouble. In Greece, this hand sign is the equivalent of showing someone the middle finger.

In some cultures, it's fine to shake a woman's hand, give her a kiss on the cheek, or even on the lips. In others, doing so might seriously offend her or brand her as a woman of loose morals.

Different cultures also have different perceptions of personal space. This can even be true of different people within the same culture, so in a situation where you don't know someone very well, or aren't sure of how much personal space they need, play it safe. According to Amanda Erickson, a Washington Post Journalist (Erickson, 2017), women tend to require more personal space than men, people from colder climates don't mind being closer than those from hot climates, and the older you are, the more space you need to not feel uncomfortable.

If you need to travel internationally for business to a country that you know little about, it's well worth considering doing some prior research, or hiring an interpreter who can assist you with understanding the cultural norms as well as the language.

Consider All Nonverbal Cues Together—Don't Jump to Conclusions Based on One

Given how much confusion non-verbal cues can sew, it would be wise to look at the big picture, and not rush to judgement. There are usually a number of cues when a person is talking to you, and they should all work together to reinforce what they are saying. If one cue is off, it might not be serious, but if a number of them are, it's time to get suspicious. The person may be intentionally trying to confuse you, or are not convinced about what they're telling you.

In western cultures, look at their face. Are they making eye contact, or are their eyes avoiding yours? What is their facial expression? A frown often denotes anger, but it can also be a sign that the person is concentrating or trying to remember.

Detectives, lawyers, and psychologists all make use of body language to help them discover the truth. It has become standard for the study of body language to be used in the training of police. Body language might not scream "I'm lying," but it will certainly tell the investigator if the person is trying to make up an answer or if they are trying to remember it. It also shows if a person is nervous, seriously afraid, angry, sad, or happy. All of these things, combined with the actual statement that the person is making need to be looked at together to ferret out what is credible and what is not.

Chapter 6:

The Power of Persuasion

Robert Cialdini (2007), a professor of psychology and celebrated author wrote about the power of persuasion in his book, *Influence: The psychology of persuasion.* He identified six different principles that help people to persuade others to their way of thinking or doing.

Here we look at each of these principles in their simplest forms and how they can be put into practice to get the outcome you're after.

The Principle of Reciprocity

The principle of reciprocity is based on the assumption that if you receive something from someone (it could be a gift or a favor), you will feel obliged to return the favor, very often in an even more generous or extravagant manner. It also recognizes that most people, on receiving a gift (or favor), whether they like it or not, feel obliged to accept it.

Certainly most of us are brought up hearing our parents say something along the lines of, "say thank you to Great Aunt Agatha for the lovely present," even if it's the most hideous, misshapen, and badly knitted sweater you've ever seen. If you said, "no thanks, I don't like it—give it to someone who does," you'd be in all sorts of trouble!

The same applies in other areas. Say you invite someone over for dinner, and a year goes by without them reciprocating. You would be disappointed, because there is an assumption that they will at least invite you over once. To not do so would be considered rude.

Have you ever gone to buy an acquaintance a birthday present, and had your partner ask you, why you are buying them a present, when they are not a particularly close friend? Your response was very likely, "because they bought me a birthday present last year, so I kind of feel I have to."

Cialdini also talks about "reciprocal concession." He gives an example of a boy scout who tried to sell him a ticket to an event for $5. He didn't want the ticket (or to attend the event), and turned him down. The boy then offered him chocolate for $1. Cialdini bought the chocolate, even though he wasn't a fan of it. His purchase was prompted by the clever young salesman offering him a 'concession' by trying to offer him something less costly, and Cialdini felt obliged to then concede himself, and bought it. The same would happen if a non-profit asked you for a monthly donation of $100. Depending on your financial situation that's not too difficult to say no to. But if they followed up with "well, could you make a once off donation, just a small one?" you may well find yourself compromising, even if you had no particular interest in that organization or its values.

You too can use this principle to improve your relationships. If you feel that your partner doesn't give you enough compliments, make an effort to pay them compliments, and you may soon find them reciprocating. Perhaps you do most of the cooking at home, and you wind up with the dishes as well. Start offering to do the dishes when your partner has cooked, sooner or later they will start feeling obliged to return the favor (if not every time, at least from time to time).

The Principle of Consistency and Commitment

According to Cialdini, people want to be consistent in their behavior, or at the very least, be seen as consistent with their behavior. What this means in terms of communication and persuasion is that if you can get a commitment out of someone publicly, or at least with one other person around as a witness, that person is more likely to follow through and honor that commitment.

It's not a magic formula to force people to do things that they don't want to do, they may still say no if they're not up for it. But if you can get them to make a commitment in front of others, the chance that they will do as they said is much higher.

This is one of the reasons why it's a really good idea to plan carefully when pitching a new idea at work. If you make it sound good and can get buy-in from the boss or some of your colleagues, even if it's just on a small scale, the chances are that they will support your project to the end, even when it takes more effort. It's also difficult, if not impossible to get people to change their minds once they have shot down your idea—they are going to try to stick to their guns. So if it's important to you, plan carefully, mold your presentation to resonate with your audience, and make a point of getting some kind of commitment at the presentation. You may not be able to force the boss to say, "yes, let's do this," but you could ask the boss whether they will commit to taking your presentation to the board, or letting you do a trial run, or provide a more detailed document on the subject. That first step of commitment is very important.

Have you ever been out with friends, and in the spirit of the evening agreed to a date with someone, only to wake up the next morning and really, really regret it? I think most people have, but if you made that commitment in front of your other friends, it is much more likely that you won't phone and make an excuse, you'll show up and struggle through the evening.

Or maybe you agreed to meet this person at the mall for coffee, now they call you and say, "hey, let's make it dinner at my place," now you're in a pickle because you initially didn't mind seeing them in public and during the day for a casual date. But you sure don't want to be having a romantic dinner with them—never mind at their home. If they had asked you to have dinner with them at home in front of your friends, you would definitely have said no. But somehow, once they have a commitment from you, they have an advantage, a "foot in the door" which makes it so much more difficult for you to wriggle out of it, even though they are the one that moved the goalpost!

The Principle of Social Proof

A simplistic explanation of Cialdini's principle of social proof is: when a person (or people) take social cues from others when they are uncertain of how to behave. Think about the first time you went out to dinner at a restaurant. You may have waited to start eating your appetizer, first checking to see what cutlery everyone else was using.

It's based on the assumption that everyone else is more confident and knows what they're doing. This has also been recognized in cases where large groups of people have been persuaded to do things that they would not normally do. It is sometimes referred to as herd or mob mentality.

Students are often roused to action through the actions of others. Once you get one person doing things your way, it's easier to convince more and more to do the same. Many freshmen who have always been shy or mild mannered, surprise their families when they are persuaded to take part in protests or political activism by seeing others do it, or wanting to be part of what is popular.

We see it in fashion all the time. Most people assume that because a fashion designer is famous and successful, that even the most ridiculous outfits they design are credible, and so they become fashionable. They must be good, because they have been created by someone who "knows best."

What this means to you as a communicator is that if you are going to try and pitch a new idea to a group of people, it's wise to test the waters beforehand and get feedback from a couple of people who you think would be supportive of the idea. Then, pitch it to your group, and ask those people who gave you positive feedback beforehand for their feedback first. Their positive opinion is likely to influence others to be more receptive. Detractors will be less likely to raise criticisms if they think that it's going to look like they're going against what they now perceive as popular opinion.

Digital marketers often use this tactic to sell more products online. They get people to review their product, or even put fake reviews online so that others, when making a decision, will look at the rave reviews and be swayed by this "social proof" that their product is better than its competitors.

The Principle of Liking

Ralph Waldo Emerson is famous for his quote "the best way to have a friend is to be one." This is the same sort of principle that Cialdini applies. The basic idea is that if you're nice to people and show that you like them, they will respond in kind.

It's a very simple concept, and not difficult to implement. If you want to improve your relationship with someone, whether it's your partner, your child or a friend, be nice to them. Pay them compliments. Genuine ones. There's no point in going around faking it, they'll see through you eventually, and find it creepy. But if someone has done something that pleases you, let them know. Say "thank you" or "that was very thoughtful." If they look good in a certain outfit, tell them. Show them that you recognize their achievements and appreciate their kindness.

This will not only encourage them to achieve more, and be kinder, but it will result in them liking you more and reciprocating this kind of behavior. If your partner is a great cook, don't take it for granted and assume that they know you like their cooking. Say, "wow, that was a great meal." People like to be recognized and appreciated, and they can't help but respond positively to someone who gives them that recognition and appreciation.

Liking is not only about compliments though. It's about physical attraction and recognizing similarities too. If you want to be taken seriously at work, try and show up looking clean and neat. You don't have to be a fashion plate, just make sure that you don't look a mess. People automatically assume if you look good, or make an effort to take care of yourself, that you have other good qualities too, like being trustworthy or reliable.

People like others who are similar to themselves. Identify similarities between yourself and your colleagues, boss, or partner, and connect with them over these things that you have in common. It will bring you closer and strengthen your ability to persuade. Again, there's no need to go overboard and lay it on thick. You can't be everyone's best friend, and faking it would be mentally draining; but when you see similarities, acknowledge them. Doing this automatically will endear you to your colleagues and improve your credibility.

When you need to give a presentation to persuade your colleagues, think of what difficulties you would experience (if you were in their shoes) and acknowledge these areas that will, very likely, be a cause of concern for them too. Say things like, "I know it's a pain to have to change the way things are done—we may all struggle with this at first, I don't look forward to XYZ, but…" and then list the benefits. This way they will feel that you're not just unilaterally forcing change. You are aware that it will take some extra effort on their part, and you will be sharing in that effort.

Authority

Authority and expertise definitely have a persuasive influence on those around you. That's why you see television commercials for toothpaste that use dentists to recommend them. Some people are authorities on subjects that they are not formally qualified in. For example, you may have a hotel manager who has a great grasp of labor laws. They are not qualified in human resource management, nor labor law, but their years of experience have resulted in considerable knowledge.

You also don't have to be an expert on, or have studied a subject to hold authority. Many models are regarded as fashion authorities, or film stars as style gurus.

The persuasive strength of authority according to Cialdini (2007) is blind obedience, He says "we are trained from birth to believe that obedience to proper authority is right, and disobedience is wrong" (p. 180).

It's important that you let your work colleagues know what your areas of authority are. I don't mean rush out beating your chest and telling everyone how wonderful you are! It's just that if you do have an area of expertise, not everyone will know, and you might find your opinions on the subject being passed over, which can be frustrating. Let them know by saying things like, "that's something that really interests me," and "I've done a lot of reading on it." Offer an opinion when a topic you are familiar with comes up for discussion.

Authority is about experience. Take for instance the hotel manager, who has done loads of research on labor law and dealt with many tricky situations. Their opinion might offer valuable insight for the fairly newly qualified human resources clerk, or they may be able to judge whether a labor consultant is good or bad at their job. If the hotel manager didn't tell the board of directors this, he or she might find that their opinions are ignored in favor of the dreadful consultant that they have contracted, or even the young human resources clerk who lacks the manager's experience. The manager would be wise to say something like, "I experienced a similar situation four years ago, and the result was…"

Scarcity

Cialdini's sixth principle of persuasion is scarcity.

Supply and demand is a principle that most people understand. When the demand for oil is high, the price is high; when demand decreases, so the price drops. This was never more apparent than during the Covid-19 pandemic when oil prices dropped to record lows.

Some things become more valuable not because there is little demand for them though, but because they are, in themselves, scarce. Think about diamonds. If diamonds were as common as the stones in your garden, you wouldn't pay a fortune for them, you'd just pick one up in the garden and fashion into a piece of jewelry. Well, to be honest, you probably wouldn't even make jewelry from it, because by becoming less scarce it would no longer be a status symbol.

The billionaire who buys a car for three million dollars is generally not buying it because he thinks it's got the strongest engine, best fuel consumption, or most comfortable seats. He is buying it because it's a limited edition, there are only a few in the world, and this is what makes it valuable. It's a status symbol, a trapping of wealth. When he drives that car, he doesn't have to say, "look at me, I'm rich," the car says it for him.

Scarcity can be deliberately created. Limited edition, handbags, shoes, and artworks are made scarce by only manufacturing a restricted number. This is done, specifically to make them more desirable and more valuable, making the designer, artist, or manufacturer more money.

The same applies to scarcity of time, which is often created in order to generate a sense of urgency e.g. something is going to be available only for a short period. Think about Black Friday offers, people line up for hours, wrangle over items, and buy things that they don't actually need, just because the price is special "just for today." In fact, Black Friday has become so popular that many retailers extend it to whole weekends, because of how much these limited time specials influence people to spend considerably more than they normally would. If those prices were dropped for the long term, you would probably think twice about whether or not you need that TV or dishwasher.

According to Cialdini (2007) "the scarcity principle trades on our weakness for shortcuts." People feel threatened by the fact that they may not have the option to get something tomorrow, so they quickly buy it today—whether they need it or not. Another Covid-19 pandemic example would be the huge rush to stock up on toilet paper worldwide. Nobody needed a whole cart-full of toilet paper, and in reality, there wasn't going to be a shortage, but once people saw others stocking up, they panicked and thought, "what if it does run out, I'd better buy now. Quickly, while it's still available."

How does this relate to communication? Well, if you need buy-in, you can use this tactic to get it by creating a sense of urgency such as, "this is a one-off offer," "we have to do this immediately if we want to achieve XYZ," or "we must act now, before our opposition thinks of it."

A Word of Caution

There is a fine line between persuasion and manipulation.

All of Cialdini's principles that we have looked at are great tactics for helping you achieve your goal when communicating. They do come with a warning however. They can be used to manipulate, and this can be extremely dangerous. Use them cautiously, responsibly, and only with the best of intentions. Before applying these tactics, give serious thought to the consequences of what you are trying to do, if it could be in any way harmful to the person or people you are using them on, don't do it. You could be held accountable for manipulation and that has a damaging effect on your relationships, career, or company's welfare.

Chapter 7:

Barriers to Effective Communication

As simple as it may seem to talk, communicate, or just say what's going on in your head, it's really way more complex than it seems. There are a number of things that can prevent you from saying what you mean, and even causing your message to be misunderstood. Some of these barriers are easily apparent, and sometimes very difficult to recognize. Fortunately, there are tactics that you can use to overcome these hurdles.

In this chapter we look at some of the common communication barriers, and how to manage them.

Stress and/or Emotion

Stress and emotion are probably two of the biggest obstacles to effective communication. When you are feeling stressed, it is not only hard to articulate what you want to say, but it also makes it just as hard to logically assess what the other person is saying and get a clear meaning, rather than one that your emotions are projecting.

If you're angry and you're having an argument with your partner, you may end up saying some hurtful things that you don't mean, or say some things that you do mean, but in a more hurtful way than you would have if you were calm. This may be because your anger stems from something that they have done or said to make you feel hurt, and you subconsciously want to make them feel as bad as you do. It goes without saying that this can only spiral into a horrible argument that leaves you both feeling hurt and unloved. If you find yourself in this situation, take a step back. Tell your partner, "I'm feeling so upset right now that I need a bit of time out to calm down, so that we can discuss this calmly. I can't order my thoughts and I'm worried I'll be mean to you." Most importantly, when having an argument, focus on the facts and how to resolve the matter, don't attack your partner's personality, neither of you stand to gain anything from a personal attack, and you can't take back words that have been spoken.

If you have received an email that has made you angry. Don't answer it immediately! Also don't leave it for days and stew over it, because that could make things even worse. Have a cup of coffee or tea, think about how you are reacting, and then ask yourself, "did this person really mean for me to feel the way I'm feeling?" Read it again to see if there is any way that you might be misinterpreting their meaning. If you can't see any kinder explanation for what they've said or how they've said it, then after calming down, respond by clarifying their intent. Let's say your boss has sent an email saying, "your department's expenditure is ridiculous." This is likely to annoy you. It's not like you've been spending money on yourself, it was all for the company, and you never spend a cent without approval. Is the boss calling you ridiculous? Suggesting you have no control or that you're wasteful?

Now you've gone back and re-read the email trying to find a kinder explanation. You might think, well they didn't actually call me ridiculous, they were referring to what the *department* is spending, but I still feel that it's a personal slight.

Now is the time to check what the boss meant. Don't go back and say "no it's not!" or "you approved every transaction!" Say, "can we chat about this? I'm feeling as if I've failed you, but I'm not sure if that is what you mean?"

I know someone who was in this situation, about 8 months into a fairly new job. She was not clear on what the budget was, and was most surprised when her boss responded to her enquiry saying, "you need to be buying more high value items." The boss was concerned that inferior products or not enough stock would have a negative impact on the company—while the poor employee who was not used to working with such a big budget was cutting corners at every opportunity out of fear of being seen as extravagant.

Pride is another emotion that can seriously hamper communication. You're presenting an idea that you're very proud of, to your colleagues, and anticipating a positive reception, maybe even a little round of applause. One of them responds in a critical way. You may find yourself too busy trying to defend your idea to explain it properly, or to listen to what they're saying. You feel deflated and lose momentum.

Maybe they have an idea that might improve your proposal or idea, and you need to hear what they say and give it proper consideration, not just reject it outright. Be aware of this, and always keep an open mind. Not all criticism is negative, and taking the best of everybody's ideas, even if it means tweaking your plan, means that your idea is going to be the best it can be, and not only the best that you could come up with. Accept that others may have valuable insights, and don't write them off as criticisms.

For some people, simply talking to more than two or three people at a time can be stressful, a few deep breaths and telling yourself that you know what you're talking about, that's why you were asked to make this address, is enough to calm the nerves. For others, a gentle herbal tranquilizer will do the trick. If you are really terrified of public speaking, and it's going to be a big event, offer to write the speech, but ask if someone else would be kind enough to say it.

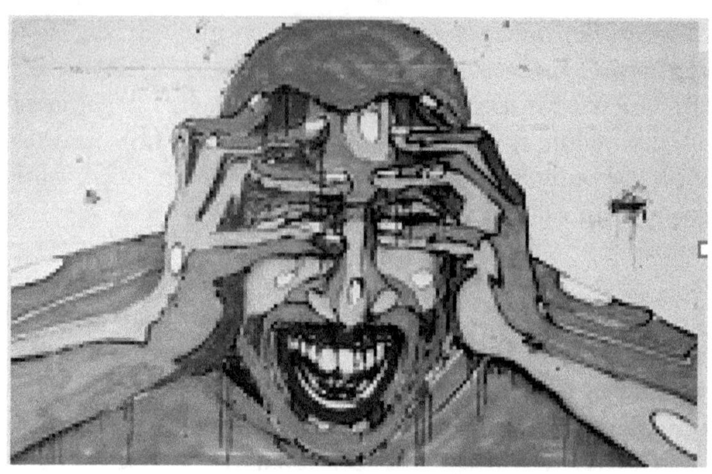

Resistance to Change

Resistance to change is a term often used in the workplace. While it's true that some people are naturally resistant to change, these are usually people who are not very confident, or have a low self-esteem. Most people however, are quite open to change. It's usually not the change itself that causes resistance, but rather the way the change is communicated, and the fear of how this is going to affect them personally.

Numerous studies have been done worldwide on the subject, and it's not surprising that almost all of them reach a common consensus: forced change receives more resistance than change in which the employees are given the opportunity to participate and add their input.

Normally change is for the better. Nobody intentionally plans changes to make their lives, company, or situation worse. But it is important as a communicator that you take the feelings and thoughts of those affected into consideration. Not necessarily to decide on whether your planned change takes place or not; but perhaps how it will take place, whether there are any better ideas out there, and if compromises could be made to keep everyone happy.

People fear change because it will take them out of their comfort zone. In a relationship, imagine a situation where you have been the breadwinner, and due to a temporary disability you are suddenly unable to work. Your partner needs to get a job, but doesn't show any sense of urgency or enthusiasm. This can be very frustrating, but it might not be because your partner is lazy and doesn't want to contribute. It may be that your partner is afraid of not doing a good job, of letting a new boss down, or even letting you down. In such an instance, it would be important to understand what is worrying your partner, and explain that they don't have to rush out and replace your full income, a more junior job will be fine with some careful budgeting, it won't be forever, and that they should be honest in interviews that they will need some on the job training.

In another scenario, if your working partner came home from work one evening and announced that they'd been offered a promotion and would be moving to another country, it could cause a major row and even signal the end of the relationship—even if you were invited to go with. But, if your partner came home and said, "I've been offered an amazing opportunity to run the operations in XYZ country, but it means relocating, let's sit down and look at the pros and cons for us and our family," you would immediately be more receptive to listening, and even willing to consider uprooting yourself.

In a business situation, this would look a little different. If you're about to make an announcement, you have already recognized the need for change, and if you've done a lot of research, you are probably not open to being talked out of it. However, you can still present it to your employees with care and consideration. Involve them as early on as is practical, if the change does not come as a surprise, they'll be more likely to accept it. Tell them that there are things that could be done more efficiently, and that you want to share your ideas on how this could be achieved, and get their feedback on it.

Your employees will want to know that you value them and their opinions, asking for their feedback tells them this. Some will also probably be afraid of losing their jobs, their position of seniority, or feel that they are not technologically savvy enough to manage the new system. Help them to feel more secure by explaining that training will be provided, and point out the benefits of the change to them—not only the benefits to the company, but for the employees themselves. Perhaps they will be able to have more flexible hours because of more efficient production, or there will be bonuses due to increased production. It could even be a simpler benefit, like not having to do as much filing.

Think carefully about employees who may feel that they will lose face as a result of this change. Maybe you're changing a system that they implemented, or bringing in a consultant who will assist with their work. You need to consider having a one on one conversation with those employees, explaining the rationale behind the change and how it will affect them personally.

Lack of Focus

There are a number of reasons why you might lose focus when communicating. If you're not interested in the subject, you could find yourself drifting off, planning what to make for dinner, or what you're going to wear on your date tonight. This is a difficult one to avoid, because you can't talk yourself into developing an interest. It will help you to keep focused however, if you take notes while the person is speaking. It keeps you engaged, even when the topic is dead boring. It also means that if the speaker should ask you a question, you will have something to reference even if your mind wasn't fully focused on their every word.

When planning your communication, plan to keep your presentation or speech interesting by including mind boggling facts and interesting or funny examples that pique the interest of your listener. Asking questions is another way to draw your audience's attention and make them focus. There is a reason why keynote speakers often start their talk with a joke or two—it helps them get everyone to concentrate on what they are saying. It also quietens the audience. If some people are still chatting amongst themselves when the speech starts, they soon stop when the rest of the room breaks into laughter, they want to be in on the joke.

Let's look at the above suggestions in practice, using two prospective openings for a talk on bees.

Example 1: Bees are a monophyletic lineage within the superfamily Apoidea. They pollinate flowers and produce small amounts of honey. They spend a lot of time in the air, and they live on average between 122 and 152 days (Wikipedia, 2019).

Example 2: It takes a lifetime for a bee to produce just *one* teaspoon of honey. To produce a kilogram of honey, bees fly the equivalent of three times around the world in airmiles. So next time you're spreading it on your morning toast, spare a thought for how precious it really is. ("Bees - fun facts," 2007).

Body Language

Body language is the non-verbal part of communication. It is made up of the message that you send (other than words) when you are talking. These can either reinforce the message that you are giving, or contradict it. When your body language contradicts the words that you are using, it causes confusion. An effective communicator not only ensures that their body language is in tune with what they are saying, but they also learn to read others' body language and consider it in context with the verbal message they are receiving.

Non-verbal cues can include tone of voice, posture, eye contact, and even movement. In writing, it comes across too—although it is quite limited—typing in capital letters or using multiple exclamation marks are the written version of "shouting." You can even denote boredom or sarcasm with an ellipsis (...). Because emails don't allow you to see the expression on the communicator's face, hear their tone of voice, or see their posture, they are the worst way to deal with conflict situations. It's too easy to misunderstand the message or read too much into it. If you have a tense conflict that needs to be resolved, it's far better to do it in person, and if that's not possible, via a video call or phone call.

If you are discussing a matter of importance, consider your posture. To look confident, lift your chin, stand up straight, and keep your arms at your sides. To look relaxed, lean back a bit in your chair and make regular eye contact. Slouching indicates a lack of confidence or a lack of interest. Failing to make eye contact can make your audience suspicious of your motives, while staring them down will be perceived as aggressive and intimidating.

Think about a situation where you were disappointed after believing that someone had been keen on your idea, only to let you down later. Was their body language aligned to their words? If your boss thanked you for your suggestion and said, "that's interesting, we'll look into it," but looked away or fiddled with their phone, the chances are that they were not really interested, and nor planning to spend much time on it.

If you are giving a presentation, look at the attitude of your audience, are they sitting up, giving you their undivided attention, or are they slouching, looking at mobiles, clicking pens, staring out the window or even doodling. In the second scenario it would be fair to judge that you have lost them. It's either time to take a break, or change the way you are presenting.

Cultural Barriers

The definition of 'culture' according to Merriam-Webster is "the customary beliefs, social forms, and material traits of a racial, religious or social group" (Merriam-Webster & Fogware Publishing, 2003).

Cultural barriers to communication are present in all facets of life. When two people of different cultures communicate, there can be an enormous disconnect. This is due not only to the beliefs and expectations of the other person, but also due to their interpretation of your beliefs and expectations—much of which is largely based on media stereotyping. It's also a problem when it comes to accents. Scottish, Welsh, and Indian accents can be particularly difficult for a second language English speaker to make out.

Idioms and points of reference differ for many cultures, and in some cultures the same English word can have a vastly different meaning. In the UK, a bag of chips is actually called crisps. Conversely, if you order chips in the UK, they would serve you french fries. This is more prevalent than you may realize, think about words like lift and elevator, pavement and sidewalk, or football and soccer.

Culture informs what you believe, what represents good or bad manners, and how we interact with each other. It's easy when you are communicating with someone from your own culture, because you will generally know all the right things to do and say to put them at ease. You can even plan your communication with a certain degree of confidence, knowing that they will understand what you are saying, not only in terms of speaking the same language, but in interpreting your body language and intention correctly.

Imagine a young Englishman from an upper-class family falling in love with a beautiful Italian girl, and their first marital argument. What she might think is just a minor storm in a teacup could very well look to him like the beginning of a divorce, it is perfectly normal in Italian culture to speak loudly and passionately, while the English (in particular, the aristocracy) are taught to subdue emotions and keep a stiff upper lip.

An American businessman would be comfortable making regular and sustained eye contact when doing a deal to reflect his honesty and trustworthiness. However, if the deal was with a Middle Eastern businesswoman, he might well find himself baffled at being shown the door halfway through his pitch. In the Middle East, direct eye contact between different genders is seen as highly flirtatious and inappropriate.

This brings us back to the point made in chapters one and two. It is really important to know your audience. Even if you don't know them personally, making sure you have some knowledge of their culture could save you from failure or an embarrassing *faux pas*.

Chapter 8

Difficult Conversations

Planning for a Difficult Conversation

The first, and probably most crucial step when planning for a difficult conversation is to not go into it with preconceived notions about the other person's intentions. I know this may sound counterproductive, having earlier said that it's important to know the person you are going to be communicating with. There is however, a difference between knowing someone (what makes them happy, sad etc.) and knowing their *intentions*.

Plan to start the conversation by finding out what their intentions and feelings are. Be willing to not only ask questions, but to actually listen to the answers. Once they've responded and you think that you know how they feel, double check. Tell them what you understood, and check if this is correct. This would go something like, "so am I correct in understanding that you feel under pressure because of XYZ?"

Be prepared for the fact that the person you are communicating with may be feeling emotional, and acknowledge the fact that you are too. After all, this wouldn't be a difficult conversation if you weren't both feeling somewhat emotional about the subject. Remind yourself to stay calm, and not read too much into what is being said. Don't let personal comments distract you from your purpose—you are having this conversation in order to resolve a problem. Make yourself focus on the facts, and help your partner or colleague to do the same by avoiding sweeping statements, exaggeration, or hurtful language.

It's important that you are clear on how they are feeling and that you acknowledge this. Acknowledging someone else's feelings or standpoint is not the same as agreeing with them. You are simply recognizing that this is how they think or feel. It is also essential that you are direct and unambiguous in letting them know how you feel. So once you understand their feelings, explain yours and why you feel the way that you do. It would be a mistake to assume that the person you are speaking to knows how you feel. This can be done without going on the attack. Don't tell them how you feel because you want to hurt them, tell them how you feel so that they can understand and sympathize with your position. Choose your words carefully, say things like "I'm sure you didn't intend for me to feel this way, but here's why I do."

Once both of your views and feelings have been made clear, and you've acknowledged or shown respect for each other's feelings, you should be ready to start looking at a solution to the problem. Be open to negotiation. This doesn't mean you have to capitulate against your better judgement for the sake of peace. That can only build further resentment, but be willing to compromise if necessary. Give a little, and take a little. Remember in Chapter 6 we looked at Cialdini's principle of reciprocity? How if you give a gift, you are likely to receive one, and probably an even more generous one at that? This is where that comes into play. Make a concession, even if it's just a small one, it will encourage the other person to do the same.

Dealing with Unplanned Difficult Conversations

In an ideal world we'd always be able to plan for difficult conversations, but the reality is that these often flare up when you least expect them. It's well worth your while having a toolkit at your disposal to help you when this happens.

It's not easy, but if you adopt a wait and see approach, and get all the facts straight before making any judgements, you should be able to steer it away from an argument and get things back on track.

Don't interrupt. Interrupting the agitated person does both of you a disservice, you are not allowing them to express themselves which will only make them angrier, and you may well embarrass yourself by jumping to conclusions and exacerbating their anger. Listen until they stop talking by themselves. Then don't say, "is that it? Are you finished?" That could come across as aggressive. Rather seek clarity and ask questions. Make sure that you have the facts straight and are properly understanding not only what they are saying, but how they are feeling. Observe their body language. Do they look or sound defensive or aggravated? Consider why they would be feeling this way, and if the reason is not immediately apparent, ask them.

Questions like, "I can see that this is important to you, let's talk about why it is impacting you in this way" go a long way. The other person will immediately calm down if they feel that you are listening to them and taking them seriously.

Check your body language. Don't fold your arms, put your hands on your hips or tap your foot. Meet their eyes and keep a relaxed position. It's very hard to fight by yourself, so just by projecting a calm demeanor (even if you don't feel it inside!) you will disarm your 'opponent.'

Sometimes just listening to someone can be enough, they may run out of steam, or realize that they are overreacting or being foolish. But if you don't hear them out, their anger may be fueled by your lack of concern for their feelings or lack of respect for their opinion. Psychologists often don't venture an opinion; they just ask pertinent questions that help their patients to work the problem out for themselves. The same approach can be very successful in a business debate or even a personal argument.

Acknowledge that both you and the other person are entitled to your own opinions and feelings, but as in a planned difficult discussion, try to deal with facts. Acknowledge the emotions, but don't spotlight them and have your discussion get derailed by them.

Perhaps you bought a new set of golf clubs, and your partner is furious. You cannot assume that they are angry because they don't think you deserve them. Deeper exploration may uncover something you weren't even aware of, perhaps your partner has been feeling a bit sidelined lately and has been desperately wishing that you could afford to go on holiday together. They haven't said anything because they didn't want to put you under financial pressure, and when you arrived home with the new golf clubs they thought, "I don't matter to my partner, they only care about golf with their friends."

Acknowledging their feelings doesn't mean you have to rush back to the store to return the clubs. You could acknowledge them by saying, "I'm sorry you feel unimportant, you're not. You mean just as much to me today as you did when we got married. I've just been under a lot of pressure at work, and the exercise and fresh air helps me to relax. I love you and will be happy to schedule some special time together. Let's have a date night."

The Basic Rules

Being Empathic

Empathy is "the feeling that you understand and share another person's experiences and emotions: the ability to share someone else's feelings" (Merriam-Webster & Fogware Publishing, 2003).

This is not to be confused with 'sympathy,' which is described as "an affinity, association, or relationship between persons or things, wherein whatever affects one similarly affects the other." Or, "inclination to think or feel alike: emotional or intellectual accord" (Merriam-Webster & Fogware Publishing, 2003).

In the case of the new golf clubs, you and your partner obviously don't feel the same way about the purchase. You have probably returned home excited and proud, and looked forward to showing your partner what a great deal you got, only to have the wind taken out of your sails by your partner's negativity.

But, if you listen and ask the relevant questions, you could develop an understanding of why your partner feels unhappy. It doesn't mean that you have to agree with your partner or even feel bad about the purchase. If you show empathy, you are willing to listen to and acknowledge their feelings.

In every difficult conversation, looking outward and acknowledging the other's feelings, is the first step to calming things down and being able to move forward. Focusing inward, and thinking only about how you feel and how hurt you are by their words, will cause them to reciprocate by doing the same. You'll quickly reach a stalemate.

Make every effort to try and understand the other person's views and feelings while still acknowledging your own.

Referring to 'I' Not 'You'

Simply changing your language from 'you' to 'I' promotes understanding, and takes the accusatory sting out of what you're saying. It allows you to express your feelings without the other person feeling judged or attacked, and so lowers their defenses.

Using 'I' neutralizes the conversation. Imagine that you have a colleague who is having an off day and snapping at everyone. Asking "what's the matter with you?" is likely to get you a negative response. But, by saying "I sense you're having a tough day, I'm happy to chat about it if you think it would help," you would be showing empathy and even a willingness to improve the situation, rather than blaming them for a bad attitude. It's often all people need, just a little understanding. You may find that the problem is not work related, but just knowing that someone cares could reduce the pressure that has been getting them down.

Perhaps you have a passive-aggressive friend. You've gone to a lot of trouble to arrange a wonderful dinner party and when you sit down to eat, they say, "I was starving, but I've passed that point now, so I probably won't eat much." Apologizing for serving the meal late would probably provide them with some satisfaction, but if it's really not that late at all, just don't rise to the bait. Either ignore the statement altogether, or say pleasantly "I wish I'd known, I would have been happy to put out some snacks for you."

What about if it's your boss who's being passive-aggressive? Every time you arrive at work in the morning, they say, "oh, look who's here, nice of you to join us…" and when you leave, they say, "going home already?" Don't take it to heart, and assume that you are at fault if you are in fact on time. The boss is probably just under stress and unhappy that they can't stick to office hours. But also, don't let it slide, it can become a bad habit and even be a bit of a power play—their way of showing who's the boss. Don't say, "you always say that, it's spiteful." Ask nicely, "would it help if I come in early tomorrow? I'd be glad to help out if you're under pressure." If they are truly under pressure and need your help, they'll be grateful for your assistance. If they are not, and are just being controlling, they should get the message. Or, if it's getting out of hand, make an appointment with them and plan carefully for the difficult conversation.

Stick to 'I' language. Keep a relaxed posture and calm tone, and say something along the lines of, "I feel hurt when you comment on my arrival and departure. It makes me feel like I'm doing something wrong, when I'm actually quite proud of my punctuality. What can I do to make it better?" or, "I'm feeling uncomfortable about arriving and leaving on time, and sensing that it's causing you some stress. Please let me know if you ever need me to put in an extra hour here or there to relieve that pressure."

Finding Common Ground

Finding common ground does not involve giving up on your principles, it is putting your focus on understanding the other person's point of view, rather than defending yours. If you make an effort to understand, you treat them with respect and show them that you value their opinion, even if it differs from yours, you have half the battle won.

Once you understand their perspective, you will be in a better position to compare the pros and cons of your different opinions. You can do this calmly and without friction. Friction comes from two people being hellbent on proving their point while not listening to the other side.

Finding common ground quite simply involves asking questions, establishing where you differ and if there are any parallels or similarities in your ideas. Again, it involves focusing on the facts and looking for solutions.

Are you seeing a pattern here? All communication benefits come from asking questions and listening to and considering the answers respectfully. You don't have to agree, you only have to show the person that you care about their opinion or feelings, that they matter.

Common ground is much easier to find if you're open and receptive to others opinions and if you treat others with respect. Sometimes that respect deteriorates over years of living or working together. It starts off with you both being comfortable with each other and not feeling that you have to put on pretenses, which is great. But, if you're not careful, after a while it can result in taking each other for granted and even worse, degenerating into disrespect.

Look at the husband who comes home hungry and tired after a long day and snipes at his wife because she hasn't even started making dinner and he wants an early night. "Is it too much to expect a meal at a decent hour?" he asks. This is going to get ugly. She's spent the day running around picking up and dropping off kids, doing laundry, paying bills, and volunteering at the school. She hasn't had a moment to herself.

If the husband had asked nicely, "what are our dinner plans?" or, said "I'm exhausted, I had a really rough day, I could really do with an early night. I see you haven't started dinner yet, would you like me to order in?" things could have gone much better. Many couples forget to hold onto the respect that they treat others with. The husband would not have spoken to his best friend that way.

The wife's best response would not be to yell back, "do you think I've been doing nothing all day? Who do you think irons your shirts—the fairies?" She should look for common ground, "I've had a crazy busy day and haven't got to it yet, and I still have to prepare the kids costumes for tomorrow's dress rehearsal. Do you want to throw something together quickly, wait for me to get to it, or order something in?"

Understanding Your Triggers

Everybody is different, and thus has different things that trigger emotion. A woman who has been having fertility issues might be triggered to feel sad when attending a friend's baby shower. Another person might feel angry when they feel disrespected, because they have low self-esteem and are constantly looking for respect from others.

Perhaps sarcasm really pushes your buttons. The important thing is to get to know your own triggers. What makes you angry, sad, or afraid? Then to analyze these situations. Perhaps you get angry when someone treats you like a fool. You feel humiliated and disrespected. You get angry with the person who is making you feel that way. But, if you think really hard about it, was the person actively trying to make you look silly, were you really being silly, or are you just so insecure about your intelligence that you read more into the situation?

Maybe you get really angry at the slightest suggestion that you might not be being truthful. Your boss says "I don't remember it like that at all," and you feel your body responding, you get hot in the face, your pulse races, and you just want to yell, "are you calling me a *liar*?" The first thing to do is hit the pause button, not respond. Ask yourself, "why am I feeling so angered by this statement?" It may just be that you really value honesty above all else, and therefore feel totally shamed and unfairly accused, because you think your honesty is in question.

Now think about your boss' intentions when they said "I don't remember it like that at all." Were they actually being confrontational? Is there a rational reason for them to be feeling confrontational? How was their tone of voice and body language? Is it possible that the boss simply doesn't recollect the incident in the same way that you do? Why did they say it? Were they trying to blame you for something, or were they just trying to puzzle out who's recollection is more accurate so that they can plan accordingly?

Knowing your triggers and understanding why they exist puts you in a position to either avoid these triggers, or speak to your boss or loved one about them, and get their help in avoiding them. It's unlikely that a person that you know and care about would intentionally say or do things to hurt you, out of the blue, without there being some build up to it.

Knowing and understanding what triggers your partner or boss is also valuable, because it will help you to keep the peace. Perhaps you know that your partner thinks you're amazing, they absolutely worship you, they don't think that they're worthy of your love. Then it would be best to avoid any signs of flirtation or even going on too much about a colleague who is 'amazing.' Your admiration for your colleague may make your partner feel threatened, even if it's completely innocent. That feeling of threat may even make your partner respond with unkind remarks about your colleague, this should be a sign that you're making them feel insecure and jealous by praising them.

It doesn't mean that you can't mention your amazing colleague, just do it with care. If you're going to say the colleague is 'super-efficient,' it might be wise to bear your partner's feelings in mind. If they stiffen up and make a negative comment, respond by telling them that you love them and why, and that your admiration for your colleague's efficiency by no means takes away from that.

Tell them that efficiency is a great asset in the office because it makes your job easier, and you like to share your successes and work stories with your partner, but that you value them for different reasons and you are not comparing. You love your partner's quirky laidback manner, and they don't need to compete with your colleague because they're your chosen person. Help them to analyze why this particular subject always causes stress, and how to deal with it.

Conclusion

By now you should have a fair grasp on the role of communication both in the workplace and in social situations. Even more importantly, you should be aware of how this can impact you and those around you both positively and negatively.

You should be able to decide what you want to say, who you are going to say it to, why you are going to be addressing them, and how you're going to deliver your message, in writing or verbally, telephonically, or in person.

With a little bit of luck, you'll also be inspired to find entertaining, captivating ways of grabbing people's attention and making sure that you hold onto it.

You can use this book to help you plan for difficult conversations, draw the best out of people, and avoid unnecessary drama and complications.

You should be able to create a safe space where your friends and associates are comfortable to talk to you without feeling judged.

In a nutshell, you should now have all the tools you need to be an effective communicator.

Have you identified your personal communication style? It may change from time to time depending on the situation and the attitude or position of the other person, but in general, what is your default style?

Have you realized that communication is not only about sending and receiving messages? It's also about considering things in context, understanding the other party and dealing with their fears and emotions, making them feel loved or valued. These are important to communication, and effective communication leads to successful relationships.

Effective communication at work will make it easier for you to understand instructions, work within boundaries, and achieve the desired outcome. It's vital for career advancement. Unless you have rare and special skills (such as a brain surgeon or rocket scientist with knowledge that very few others have) you will find that success and promotion are firmly linked to your ability to communicate. By this I don't mean public speaking, I mean engaging with others even one on one.

Why? Well because if you're an effective communicator, you inspire trust and foster good relationships. You are supportive and can get the best out of your team.

At home, your effective communication can create a happy and loving environment. Your children should feel safe to talk to you about their fears and your partner should feel secure and loved. Have you heard the expression "happy wife, happy life"? Well, it works both ways. It's hard for one partner to be happy when the other is not, and the key to happiness lies, at a basic level, in feeling secure and cared for.

Have you ever met one of those old couples who've been together for so long they can complete each other's sentences, and can cheerfully sit in silence together for hours on end? It's not some major stroke of luck that put the right person in their path at the right time—even though they may think so. It's the result of years of considerate, respectful, and empathic communication. It's from taking the time and trouble to understand themselves and each other when things weren't going well, and making the effort to find common ground.

Don't be disappointed if things still go wrong, and misunderstandings still happen. There are far too many complicated and diverse personalities, cultures, differing needs, and environments in the world for every communication to go smoothly.

Just know that you are not responsible for everybody else's feelings and reactions. You are responsible for yours. When things do go awry, just dig in your mental toolkit, distance yourself for a moment to assess the situation; gather your thoughts and calm your mind if one of your triggers has been pressed.

Refocus with the facts and intention of the other communicator in mind. Get clarity from the other person as to why they are responding with unhappiness, and see if you can find common ground.

If you can do all of that, and show that you are open to listening and supporting the person you're talking to you, are likely to achieve so much more than if you shut them out and defend your point of view.

Understanding what makes people tick is the first step in being able to harness your powers of persuasion. But use these powers kindly, they should be used for good and not bad. Don't manipulate for the sake of it, consider your motives carefully and be true to yourself and those around you.

Use your newfound skills to make your world a better place, hone them and polish them and you will be delighted with the unexpected benefits they bring.

References

Alexandra Mirgheş, A. (n.d.). Unsplash Photo Community. Retrieved from: https://unsplash.com/@alexandramirghes?utm_source=unsplash&utm_medium=referral&utm_content=creditCopyText

auf der Heide, K. (n.d.). Unsplash Photo Community. Retrieved from: https://unsplash.com/@kadh?utm_source=unsplash&utm_medium=referral&utm_content=creditCopyText

Bees – fun facts. (2007, June 30). Science Learning Hub. https://www.sciencelearn.org.nz/resources/2002-bees-fun-facts

Buitenwerf, F. (n.d.). Unsplash Photo Community. Retrieved from: https://unsplash.com/@iamfelicia?utm_source=unsplash&utm_medium=referral&utm_content=creditCopyText

Cialdini, R. B. (2007). *Influence : the psychology of persuasion*. Collins.

D-X, C. (n.d.). Unsplash Photo Community. Retrieved from: https://unsplash.com/@cdx2?utm_source=unsplash&utm_medium=referral&utm_content=creditCopyText

Erickson, A. (2017, April 24). Analysis | What 'personal space' looks like around the world. *The Washington Post*. https://www.washingtonpost.com/news/worldviews/wp/2017/04/24/how-close-is-too-close-depends-on-where-you-live/

Gupta, B. (n.d.). Unsplash Photo Community. Retrieved from: https://unsplash.com/@bhuvii?utm_source=unsplash&utm_medium=referral&utm_content=creditCopyText

Hill, R. (n.d.). Unsplash Photo Community. Retrieved from: https://unsplash.com/@randalynhill?utm_source=unsplash&utm_medium=referral&utm_content=creditCopyText

Leung, J. (n.d.). Unsplash Photo Community. Retrieved from: https://unsplash.com/@ninjason?utm_source=unsplash&utm_medium=referral&utm_content=creditCopyText

Merriam-Webster., & Fogware Publishing. (2003). *Merriam-Webster's collegiate dictionary & thesaurus.* United States Of America: Merriam-Webster, Inc.

Novak, M. C. (2019). 4 Types of Communication Styles (+Which One Is the Most Effective). G2.com. https://learn.g2.com/communication-styles

Schwartz, M. (n.d.). Unsplash Photo Community. Retrieved from: https://unsplash.com/@cadop?utm_source=unsplash&utm_medium=referral&utm_content=creditCopyText

Tejedor, A. B. (n.d.). Unsplash Photo Community. Retrieved from: https://unsplash.com/@healing_photographer?utm_source=unsplash&utm_medium=referral&utm_content=creditCopyText

The Myers-Briggs Company. (2017). Myers-Briggs Type Indicator® (MBTI®) | Official Myers Briggs Personality Test. Themyersbriggs.com. https://www.themyersbriggs.com/en-US/Products-and-Services/Myers-Briggs

Tumisu. (n.d.). Retrieved from Pixabay website: https://pixabay.com/illustrations/divorce-separation-relationship-908742/

Wikipedia Contributors. (2019, February 21). *Bee.* Wikipedia. https://en.wikipedia.org/wiki/Bee